Dyadic Developmental Psychotherapy

Dyadic Developmental Psychotherapy

Essential Practices and Methods

Arthur Becker-Weidman, PhD

Foreword by Daniel A. Hughes, PhD

JASON ARONSON

Lanham • Boulder • New York • Toronto • Plymouth, UK

Published by Jason Aronson
A division of Rowman & Littlefield Publishers, Inc.
A wholly owned subsidiary of The Rowman & Littlefield Publishing Group, Inc.
4501 Forbes Boulevard, Suite 200, Lanham, Maryland 20706
http://www.rowmanlittlefield.com

Estover Road, Plymouth PL6 7PY, United Kingdom

British Library Cataloguing in Publication Information Available

Library of Congress Cataloging-in-Publication Data

Becker-Weidman, Arthur, 1953–
Dyadic developmental psychotherapy : essential practices and methods / Arthur Becker-Weidman ; foreword by Daniel A. Hughes.
p. ; cm.
Includes bibliographical references and index.
ISBN 978-0-7657-0793-2 (cloth : alk. paper) — ISBN 978-0-7657-0795-6 (electronic)
1. Attachment behavior in children. 2. Child psychotherapy. 3. Family psychotherapy. I. Title.
[DNLM: 1. Family Therapy—methods. 2. Developmental Disabilities—therapy. 3. Family Relations. WM 430.5.F2]
RJ507.A77B43 2011
618.92'89156—dc22 2010033259

∞™ The paper used in this publication meets the minimum requirements of American National Standard for Information Sciences—Permanence of Paper for Printed Library Materials, ANSI/NISO Z39.48-1992.

Printed in the United States of America

Contents

Foreword

Dyadic Developmental Psychotherapy (DDP) is a model of psychological treatment that is based on principles that derive from attachment theory and research. The goal of these principles is to facilitate the development of the attachment relationship between a child and his parent or caregiver, while resolving any trauma or loss that had impaired such development. DDP is similar to many models of psychotherapy in that it is grounded in the therapeutic relationship, including the experience of empathy, which is probably the therapeutic factor that has the greatest "evidence-base" of all the factors that have been studied. Where DDP may differ from many "relationship-based" models of psychotherapy is its specific emphasis on the attachment relationship for its organizing principle. In DDP the therapist is clear—not ambiguous—about the impact that the client is having on the therapist. In DDP the therapist is actively engaged in experiencing and communicating to his clients the impact that they are having on him. The therapist is actively discovering strengths and vulnerabilities of the client that lie under the client's behaviors (or symptoms) and in so doing enabling the client to discover these same qualities. In DDP the therapist is creating safety for the client through his consistency, predictability, and boundaries, as well as his active expression of the attitude of PACE (Playful, Accepting, Curious, and Empathic).

All of these features are also central in the infant or older child's attachment security that develops with his parent or caregiver. While DDP strives to have the client experience the therapist's active presence in a manner similar to how a child experiences the presence of the child's parent or caregiver, even more importantly, DDP strives to develop the child-parent relationship along the same principles. For this reason, DDP is primarily a model of family therapy, not individual therapy. The DDP therapist chooses the individual treatment modality only when the child or adolescent does not live with a caregiver who is committed and able to become a source of attachment security for the child or adolescent.

This book, *Dyadic Developmental Psychotherapy: Essential Practices and Methods* by Dr. Arthur Becker-Weidman represents one more contribution that he has made to the development of DDP. Becker-Weidman's research studies serve as important building blocks to the knowledge base that is crucial to the development of a new model of psychotherapy. Other empirical or experimental clinical practice research is occurring in the United States and United Kingdom with the hope that it will serve as the foundation for larger, university-based research in the years ahead. Becker-Weidman and Deborah Shell have co-edited two important books on DDP as it is being applied to treatment and parenting interventions by a number of clinicians trained in this treatment model. Finally, Becker-Weidman has played a central role in the development of Dyadic Developmental Psychotherapy Institute (DDPI), which has established and maintains principles for insuring that DDP is practiced in a manner that represents a valid and reliable application of its core principles and interventions. DDPI offers a certification process for clinicians who want to participate in the DDP community as therapists, consultants, and trainers.

In *Dyadic Developmental Psychotherapy: Essential Practices and Methods*, Becker-Weidman provides many clinical examples of his application of DDP with a variety of clients. These examples are rich in therapeutic dialogue that is crucial if clinicians are to truly understand the heart of DDP. The DDP therapist assumes a clear and active stance to insure that affective-reflective dialogue occurs throughout the session and the treatment process as a whole, believing that such dialogue facilitates the attachment relationship and the development of a coherent autobiographical narrative. Children who have experienced developmental trauma and attachment disorganization have great difficulty initiating and maintaining such dialogues, which in turns makes it difficult for them to become successfully engaged in and to benefit from psychotherapy. The DDP therapist leads the child and his parents into such dialogues, insuring that the child's narrative will be explored with PACE and that the intersubjective experience and exploration will lead to the co-creation of new, integrated meanings for the past traumatic events.

Dyadic Developmental Psychotherapy: Essential Practices and Methods highlights Becker-Weidman's perspective on sequential phases (developing and maintaining the alliance, exploration, integration, and healing) within DDP treatment. It is important for the reader to remember Becker-Weidman's following comment: "These phases are presented in a discrete manner for pedagogic purposes here. In practice, the phases overlap and the therapist and family move through treatment, and circle back and forth among the states even within one session."

DDP is grounded in the subjective and intersubjective experience of the therapist and client(s) within the treatment sessions. DDP interventions facilitate clarifying, deepening, and integrating such experiences into a coherent narrative. It is crucial that our efforts to organize such experiences conceptually facilitate this experiential process rather than distort it through making the experience fit the conceptual model. Therapists might reflect on Becker-Weidman's emphasis on sequential phases with respect to whether it brings additional clarity and organization to their own experience of DDP. Also, these phases are similar to those presented in trauma-focused therapies. It is important for the DDP clinician to remember that there are various important differences between DDP and those therapies, even though we might be using the same terms. For example, in DDP the therapist—utilizing principles of attachment and intersubjectivity—is likely to be able to develop and maintain the therapeutic alliance with all members of the family more quickly and deeply than is the more traditional therapist who adopts a more neutral stance and is ambiguous regarding the impact that the family members are having on the therapist.

Becker-Weidman describes the importance of the parent or caregiver's commitment to the child if he or she is to serve as an attachment figure for their child in the process of developing safety, healing, and a coherent narrative. He makes the reader aware of the important research of Mary Dozier with regard to the commitment of the foster parent if the child is to truly benefit from a foster placement. The DDP therapist needs to assess the parent or caregiver's level of commitment before asking the child to rely more fully upon that relationship. If the DDP therapist encourages the child to rely on a commitment that is not present, the therapy will only produce another traumatic experience for the child.

I believe that this work, along with the other two books co-edited by Arthur Becker-Weidman and Deborah Shell, will assist therapists in understanding DDP from the perspectives of other therapists experienced in DDP. At the same time, this work will hopefully encourage therapists to further develop their own perspectives which they may share within the safety and intersubjective exploration that exists within the DDP community. Dyadic Developmental Psychotherapy is a method of treatment that is grounded in the subjective and intersubjective experiences of the therapist and client. All of us practicing this attachment-focused form of treatment must reflect upon these experiences in order to better understand and develop and communicate them to others. I believe that Becker-Weidman's work will definitely stand with contributions of other DDP therapists in the years to come in insuring the place of DDP within the therapeutic community, and especially that part of the community that is influenced by attachment theory and research.

Daniel A. Hughes

Acknowledgments

There are a number of people whose guidance, help, and support helped make this book possible.

Dan Hughes has been wonderfully encouraging as I tried to write about his treatment. I value Dan's opinions and thinking. I enjoyed writing an article (Becker-Weidman & Hughes, 2008) with him a few years ago and have always learned from his insights. I consider Dan a friend and a mentor. Dan's support and teaching have been a source of enormous professional growth for me, which is reflected in this book.

My friends and colleagues, Deb Shell and Robert Spottswood, have been a source of help and guidance in this process. I always knew I could turn to them to better understand difficult experiences and that I could count on them for sound advice and guidance.

There were a number of board members of the Dyadic Developmental Psychotherapy Institute and fellow certified Dyadic Developmental Psychotherapy therapists whose comments on the Dyadic Developmental Psychotherapy Institute's listserv helped me clarify and sharpen my thinking. Their time and contributions made this a better text.

Jeanne Koch, who was an intern at the Center for Family Development while I was working on this book, transcribed many of the clinical examples in this book from my extensive collection of training DVDs. Thanks to her, this book is rich in clinical examples that illustrate various components, stages, and principles of Dyadic Developmental Psychotherapy.

A NOTE ON THE TRANSCRIPTS

While the transcripts and dialogues presented in this book are based on actual client sessions, all names and identifying information has been altered so that the identities of the people have been disguised and their anonymity and confidentiality preserved. All transcripts are from DVD recorded treatment sessions for which client informed consent and permission to use the sessions for training purposes have been obtained. The material has been altered in accordance with the American Psychological Association's standards regarding publication.

Chapter 1

Introduction

Dyadic Developmental Psychotherapy is an effective, evidence-based, and empirically validated treatment. The development of Dyadic Developmental Psychotherapy is described in detail by its originator, Dr. Daniel Hughes (2005/2008). Hughes developed this model over several years, beginning in the late 1980s. Hughes continues to develop the model, including the expansion of the model from the treatment of abused and neglected children in foster and adoptive homes to a comprehensive model of family treatment (Hughes, 2007, in press). Dyadic Developmental Psychotherapy continues to evolve as research, described below, and clinical practice have led the way toward a richer and deeper understanding of the factors that help families and children. As the creator of this model, Hughes has written several texts that describe this model (Hughes, 2004; Hughes, 2006; Hughes, 2007; Hughes, in press). These texts present Dyadic Developmental Psychotherapy as a model for treatment that is firmly grounded in shared experiences and the healing power of emotions within the therapeutic setting. The model has now been extended by Hughes and is also described as Attachment Focused Family Therapy because of its broad applicability to a variety of settings and for a variety of clients, (Hughes 2007). Dyadic Developmental Psychotherapy can be thought of as the application of this approach to families where disorders of attachment and trauma are central difficulties.

As I was writing up the results of my second follow-up study demonstrating the effectiveness of Dyadic Developmental Psychotherapy four years after treatment ended (Becker-Weidman, 2006b), I began thinking about developing a comprehensive guide to the practice, principles, and application of Dyadic Developmental Psychotherapy as most easily presented to those interested in learning about this approach and for current practitioners.

I continued to think about this as I expanded my training of therapists in a Master Class offered regularly in the United States and overseas. Hughes has written a workbook (Hughes, in press) that will function as a core text for those taking workshops and training that can lead to certification as a Dyadic Developmental Psychotherapist by the Dyadic Developmental Psychotherapy Institute. It occurred to me that while there were a number of good texts about Dyadic Developmental Psychotherapy (Becker-Weidman & Shell, 2005/2008; Hughes, 2006; Hughes 2007; Hughes, in press), a detailed exposition of the approach would complement those texts if it were to describe the major components of Dyadic Developmental Psychotherapy and how those components are integrated and used differently within various phases of treatment and with different types of families. While the concept of phase is not intrinsic or inherent to Dyadic Developmental Psychotherapy, the participants of my classes have found the phase concept to be a useful construct in thinking about this approach. This book is intended to provide students and practitioners of Dyadic Developmental Psychotherapy, from beginners to those certified as a Dyadic Developmental Psychotherapy therapist, consultant, or trainer, a detailed guide to the practice of Dyadic Developmental Psychotherapy. In addition, it is hoped that this book will increase consistency in the application of the model by individuals who are using Dyadic Developmental Psychotherapy in their practice and for research. In some ways this book is an adjunct or support to the work of the Dyadic Developmental Psychotherapy Institute, which was founded in 2008, to ensure continued integrity to the model of treatment developed by Hughes. Integrity in the application of the model facilitates reliability of delivery across a spectrum of practitioners and facilitates the highest quality research.

After absorbing the material in this book the reader should have a clear understanding of the practice of Dyadic Developmental Psychotherapy, and how one can practically use it. Advanced clinicians will find this useful to develop a more focused understanding of the work. Therapists, parents, residential treatment staff, social workers, psychologists, child welfare workers, and many others should also find this book useful. It will provide them with a deeper understanding of the practice of Dyadic Developmental Psychotherapy and, as a treatment manual, with as explicit a road map as I can define, given the need to be acutely responsive to the inner life of the clients in the room in the moment. The practice of Dyadic Developmental Psychotherapy is both art and science. The use of self is central to this approach, and one should be able to implement Dyadic Developmental Psychotherapy in a manner consistent with individual personality, history, and pattern of attachment; that is the art. This book will attempt to provide a framework for using one's self therapeutically within the context of Dyadic Developmental Psychotherapy; that is the science.

RESEARCH BASE

Dyadic Developmental Psychotherapy is an effective, evidence-based (Craven & Lee, 2006) and empirically validated treatment. Craven & Lee (2006) determined that Dyadic Developmental Psychotherapy is a supported and acceptable treatment (category 3 in a six-level system). However, their review was only based on results from a partial preliminary presentation of an ongoing follow-up study, subsequently completed and published in 2006. This study compared the results of Dyadic Developmental Psychotherapy with other forms of treatment, "usual care," one year after treatment ended. A second study extended these results to four years after treatment ended. Based on the Craven & Lee classifications (Saunders et al. 2004), inclusion of those studies would have resulted in Dyadic Developmental Psychotherapy being classified as an evidence-based category 2, "Supported and probably efficacious." Since the development of Dyadic Developmental Psychotherapy, there have been two empirical studies demonstrating the effectiveness of Dyadic Developmental Psychotherapy published by this author (Becker-Weidman, 2006a, Becker-Weidman, 2006b). These two studies each had a sample size of 64.

The first study (Becker-Weidman, 2006a) compared two groups of children who met the criteria for Reactive Attachment Disorder and Complex Trauma. The experimental group received Dyadic Developmental Psychotherapy at The Center for Family Development, while the control group received other standardized treatments by other qualified professionals at other clinics. The two groups were matched and were not significantly different on a variety of variables including age, gender, length of time in placement or adoption, and their pre-treatment scores on the Child Behavior Checklist (CBCL) (Ackenbach, 1991) and various other demographic variables. Both groups of children had scores in the clinical range on the CBCL before treatment. One year after treatment ended, the children in the experimental group (Dyadic Developmental Psychotherapy treatment) had post-test scores on all scales of the CBCL that were in the normal range and that were statistically significantly different from their pre-test scores. The children in the control group had post-test scores that remained in the clinical range and there were not statistically significantly different from their pre-test scores.

The second study (Becker-Weidman, 2006b) followed the children for four years after treatment ended. This study found that the children who had received Dyadic Developmental Psychotherapy continued to have CBCL scores in the normal range, remaining statistically significantly lower than their pre-test CBCL scores. Children in the experimental group, who actually continued to receive other treatment from other providers, not only had CBCL scores that remained in the clinical range, but on four of the CBCL scales their scores were statistically significantly worse: Anxious/Depressed, Attention Problems, Rule-Breaking Behavior, and Aggressive Behavior.

Tables 1.1 and 1.2 summarize the results of the two empirical studies cited above.

Dyadic Developmental Psychotherapy is an affect-focused family therapy based on Attachment Theory (Bowlby 1980, 1988; Holmes, 1993) and draws on the best of several previously established, evidence-based approaches, methods, and techniques that have a strong evidence base. Dyadic Developmental Psychotherapy uses a variety of interventions and methods with a well-established foundation. For example, Dyadic Developmental Psychotherapy is consistent with the basic principles of effective treatment for complex trauma (Cook et al., 2003, 2005). Cook et al. identify six core components of complex trauma interventions: "safety, self-regulation, self reflective information processing, traumatic experience integration, relational engagement, and positive affect enhancements" (Cook et al, 2005 p. 395). Dyadic Developmental Psychotherapy emphasizes each of these six core components. Specific components, methods, and principles of Dyadic Developmental Psychotherapy that have good empirical support and are shared with other treatment approaches (Orlinsky, Grawe, & Parks, 1994) include the following:

1. Affect arousal, a focus on problems of living and on core personal relationships have been shown to be important for positive outcomes for treatment.
2. Articulating how the past may continue to effect present behavior, emotions, and interpretation has been found to be an effective mode of intervention.
3. Forming and maintaining a therapeutic bond. This is a core component of Dyadic Developmental Psychotherapy. The therapeutic attitude of PACE (Playful, Accepting of the emotions and experience of the other, Curious about how the person experiences the world and the meaning the person ascribes to events, Empathy for the person) is designed specifically to help facilitate the therapeutic relationship. There is a significant positive association between outcome and the therapeutic bond (66 percent of the studies with an effect size of at least .25 in one quarter of the studies, p. 308 of Orlinsky et al., 1994). In looking at the therapist's contribution

Table 1.1. Statistical Analysis of Treatment Group

	Pre-test		Post-test				2nd post-test		
Measure	*Mean*	*SD*	*Mean*	*SD*	*t-value*	*p-value*	*Mean*	*SD*	*t-test prob.*
CBCL *syndrome scale scores*									
Withdrawn	65	11.8	54	6.0	4.897	<.0001	56	6	.008
Anxious/depressed	62	10.5	58	8.1	2.665	.006	58	5	.006
Social problems	67	9.7	59	5.5	4.376	<.0001	56	5	.001
Thought problems	68	9.5	65	3.9	6.133	<.0001	60	8	.02
Attention problems	72	12.5	57	6.1	5.836	<.0001	57	6	<.0002
Rule-breaking behavior	69	6.9	53	3.8	12.181	<.0001	52	3	<.0001
Aggressive behavior	71	9.1	55	4.5	10.576	<.0001	54	4	<.0001

Table 1.2. Statistical Analysis of Control Groups

	Pre-test		Post-test				2nd post-test		
Measure	*Mean*	*SD*	*Mean*	*SD*	*t-value*	*p-value*	*Mean*	*SD*	*t-test prob.*
CBCL *syndrome scale scores*									
Withdrawn	65	10.5	63	9.45	1.427	.16	71	49	.18
Anxious/depressed	62	10.6	60	10.3	1.060	.30	70	10	.03
Social problems	64	11.1	65	11.25	-0.854	.40	65	2	.5
Thought problems	63	8.6	62	8.1	0.984	.33	67	8	.8
Attention problems	68	11.9	66	10.8	0.927	.36	77	9	.02*
Rule-breaking behavior	67	7.4	66	9/6	1.8691	.07	81	4	.02*
Aggressive behavior	70	10.2	68	9.4	0.919	.37	81	4	.02*

* Statistically significant

to the therapeutic bond, a significant positive association with outcome was found: "The therapist's contribution was positively associated with outcome 67% of the time and never negatively implicated" (p. 321). "The strongest evidence linking process to outcome concerns the therapeutic bond or alliance" (p. 360).

4. Acceptance. This is a significant dimension of the practice of Dyadic Developmental Psychotherapy. Therapist affirmation (acceptance, non-possessive warmth, or positive regard) was found to be a significant factor in positive therapeutic outcome.

Overall such factors as empathy, the capacity for reflection, intersubjective sharing of affect, the therapeutic alliance, furthering reflection, deepening emotional processing, enhancing adaptive skills, developing and maintaining the therapeutic bond, therapist affirmation, communication attunement, and the bond of relatedness between therapist and patient are all important factors in psychotherapy outcome and are all important elements of Dyadic Developmental Psychotherapy.

The first section of this book describes places to begin, such as the importance of getting a thorough assessment and what is an attachment perspective and how this can explain behavior that otherwise may seem incomprehensible. While getting a thorough assessment is neither unique nor intrinsic to Dyadic Developmental Psychotherapy, I do consider it good practice and so include it in this book.

The second section of this book describes fourteen major components of Dyadic Developmental Psychotherapy. These components include:

Therapist use of self
Process focused: It's about connections not compliance
PLACE & PACE (Playful, Loving, Accepting, Curious, Empathic & Playful, Accepting, Curious, Empathic)
Intersubjectivity
Reflective Capacity
Affective/Reflective dialogue
Commitment
Insightfulness
Coherent Narrative
Co-regulation of emotions
Co-creation of meaning
Follow-lead-follow
Interactive repair
Nonverbal-verbal dialogue

I then describe my thinking on phases of treatment as applied to the practice of Dyadic Developmental Psychotherapy. This provides a framework for understanding which elements of Dyadic Developmental Psychotherapy may be more salient at that point in treatment. This chapter describes each phase of treatment in detail and the mix of Dyadic Developmental Psychotherapy components that may have more salience at that phase when using Dyadic Developmental Psychotherapy. Clinical examples are used to illustrate various points. The concept of phases is used as a teaching tool and as an application of attachment theory to thinking about Dyadic Developmental Psychotherapy, which is grounded in attachment theory. As used in this book, the phases should not be construed as a rigid set of steps that occur in a linear or prescribed manner. The reader can think of phases in the same way that phases of the moon are viewed. The whole remains present, but in different phases, different sections of that whole are highlighted and appear more prominent. The use of phases to think about practice can be experienced as one aspect of the reflective part of the therapist's own internal affective/reflective dialogue. The therapist must experience the clients in the moment (the affective dimension) while being able to reflect on this experience and make sense of it (the reflective dimension). The concept of phases can aid in this reflection. Feedback from teaching workshops, seminars, and classes suggests that the concept of phases can be useful when learning about Dyadic Developmental Psychotherapy. These phases are: building the alliance (secure base), maintaining the alliance, exploration, integration, and healing. The phases occur in a cyclic sequential fashion and have substantial overlap. A beginning alliance and exploration, integration, and healing can begin with the first meeting, or may be spread out over an extended period of time. Exploration, integration, and healing occur in a cyclical manner, deepening as treatment proceeds.

Chapter 2

First Things First

Before beginning treatment a thorough and comprehensive assessment of the family, parents, and child should occur. While this is not an essential or unique element of Dyadic Developmental Psychotherapy, it is generally good practice and so is presented in this chapter as an "adjunct" to the practice of Dyadic Developmental Psychotherapy. The material in this chapter is largely a reflection of my own professional experience and thinking about what constitutes a thorough assessment and evaluation. What I present in this chapter are my views on assessment and my application of various principles of Dyadic Developmental Psychotherapy to the assessment process. As you will see, the focus is on what is causing behavior, what is the intention, what is driving action; our primary concern is the meaning of the behavior—Causes not Symptoms are the focus. Children who have experienced chronic early maltreatment within a caregiving relationship, Complex Trauma (Cook, Blaustein, Spinazolla, & van der Kolk, 2003; Cook, Spinazzola, Ford, Lanktree, Blaustein, Cloitre, et al., 2005), can have impairment in a variety of domains with symptoms that, while looking quite similar, have quite distinct causes and, therefore, require different treatments. Since we treat causes, it is vital to have a thorough assessment. Complex Trauma can cause pervasive difficulties across multiple domains. Effective treatment interventions require that we understand the underlying nature and drivers of the problems we observe.

A comprehensive assessment should consider the family, parents, and child. It should address the various domains that can be affected by Complex Trauma (attachment, behavioral regulation, emotional regulation, biology, cognition, dissociation and defenses, and self-esteem). A comprehensive evaluation should screen for a variety of issues such as prenatal exposure to chemicals, neuropsychological impairments, sensory-integration issues, patterns of attachment, and mental health issues, among other areas. A very detailed description of a three-session model for assessment can be found in Becker-Weidman, 2005/2008 and Becker-Weidman, 2007.

For example, let me describe for you a child as she was described to me. Nine-year-old Jessica often "does not listen," she is "oppositional" and "defiant," frequently refusing to do what her parents or teachers ask her to do. When she does "comply," she repeatedly will only do some of what she was asked to do. Her parents and teachers experience her "passive-aggressive" and "oppositional defiant behaviors," as upsetting and very frustrating.

Implicit in the above example are the assumptions of the adults about what is motivating or causing Jessica's behavior. The words, phrases, and "diagnoses," what I call their theory of her behavior, imply that Jessica is acting purposefully. This "hypothesis" of why Jessica is acting as she does naturally leads to the adults feeling a certain way toward her (frustrated, irritated, upset) and then acting accordingly. Now, their "hypothesis" could be right. On the other hand, an evaluation might reveal that Jessica's history of chronic early maltreatment within a caregiving relationship causes her to be fearful of adult demands because her past experiences have shown her that adult demands are hurtful or bad for her. In this instance, if this is true, then her behavior now makes sense. She is not motivated by trying to be difficult, she is motivated by fear. In addition, we may find that Jessica has some central auditory processing dysfunction so that her ability to process requests is impaired. In this instance, her behavior is caused by her difficulty processing auditory information and sequencing. Finally, we may find that Jessica's developmental age is substantially below her chronological age, as is not infrequently the case with such children (Becker-Weidman, 2009). In this instance, her behavior is caused by our asking her to do things that she may not be capable of doing because we are expecting her to act like a nine-year-old when she is actually developmentally younger than that.

So, as you can see, our theory of behavior dramatically affects how we feel about the person and then how we act toward that person. A comprehensive assessment can help us determine what may be driving the behavior and then help us determine the most therapeutic course of action.

ASSESSING THE FAMILY AND PARENTS

Assessing the family is important since this is the venue within which most of the healing aspects of treatment occur. It is of paramount importance that the family be a physically, emotionally, and psychologically safe place for all involved. "Safety First" is a basic tenant of trauma treatment and applies to the application of Dyadic Developmental Psychotherapy. During the three session model of assessment previously mentioned, the clinician can be evaluating the extent to which each family member involved in treatment feels safe and the extent to which each adult can provide safety. In a later chapter I will describe some of the elements of Dyadic Developmental Psychotherapy that are involved in creating a safe, secure base, and how weak areas can be strengthened. Specifically, we know that the best predictor of placement stability is parent commitment (Dozier, & Lindhiem, 2006). Commitment is the "L" in PLACE (Loving). Other important factors are the parent(s) state of mind with respect to attachment (Dozier, Stovall, Albus, & Bates, 2001), insightfulness (Koren-Karie, Oppenheim, Dolev, Sher, & Etzion-Carasso, 2002, Oppenheim, & Koren-Karie, 2002), reflective ability, and sensitivity. The parent's ability to create concordant intersubjective experiences is grounded in these factors. The provision of responsive, sensitive, attuned caring requires a care-giver who is insightful, committed, has a well developed reflective ability, and a secure state of mind with respect to attachment.

ASSESSING PARENTS

Why do we bother assessing parents? Complex trauma and disorders of attachment are relational problems and so they require relationship-based treatment. The parents or primary caregivers are central to treatment outcome and success. They are the primary healing element. Once this concept is clearly understood, then it becomes clear that a thorough assessment of the primary caregivers' capacities, abilities, and limitations is essential for treatment to succeed. The primary caregivers' capacities, abilities, and limitations are the best predictor of treatment outcome; better than "how disturbed" is the child. Parents are the keystone of treatment and treatment success. By understanding the primary caregiver's capacities, abilities, and limitations in the important areas of attachment, insightfulness, commitment, and reflective function we are better able to plan our treatment.

Parents whose own past traumas are still affecting their parenting in a negative way will require more support and help by the clinician before beginning the family components of treatment. In addition, the pace of treatment will have to be slower to take into account the parent(s) issues and to address those in a sensitive manner so that a therapeutic alliance can be developed. Creating a secure base with these parents will take longer since often their capacity to trust and engage in concordant intersubjective experiences has been damaged by their past negative experiences with their own caregivers. The clinician will need to take more time to develop an alliance with these parents. It is vital for good outcomes that the clinician be able to build a trusting alliance with the primary caregivers and create a secure base within which obstacles to treatment can be explored.

I have found that sometimes, in training therapists, I hear, "if only the parents would just get it, things would be fine; this is a great kid." While this is understandable, it does represent a lack of empathy by the clinician for the parent. It is essential to develop empathy for the parents and recognize that while their intentions are usually good their actions may not be. Often you will find that the parent(s) feel some shame about their past actions but don't know what else to do. Developing an alliance with the primary caregivers, empathy, and a secure base will allow the parents to feel safe enough to explore their intentions and actions and develop new and more effective ways to enact their intentions. Within a relationship with the therapist in which the parents experience safety, understanding, and acceptance the parents will be better able to explore the potential mismatch between their intentions and their actions.

We all have "buttons" that can be pressed by others; but it is important to remember who owns and controls the button: you do. Helping parents understand this very important concept is often central to helping the parents create a healing PLACE at home. In many ways the children we work with are "relationship phobic." They've had all sorts of experiences that have taught them, experientially, that relationships, intimacy, and emotional closeness are dangerous and not rewarding. We all have a degree of intimacy and emotional distance/closeness that feels comfortable. In relationships we maintain that "feels good distance." The children we work with have had experiences that have taught them to rely on themselves and to keep a degree of emotional intimacy (distance) that is much larger than what most of us are comfortable with in our relationships; they are relationships phobic. Like we all do, these children find ways to maintain the degree of intimacy that feels familiar to them, which in the case of children with complex trauma and disorders of attachment, is quite a limited degree of intimacy. So, what happens is that the child does all sorts of things and then finds that one set of actions creates the degree of intimacy with which the child is familiar; the child finds your button and pushes it. Once we

Oscar and Maria adopted Karl when he was six years old. After four years in an abusive home, Karl had the scars on his back and legs to show why he found it difficult to trust adults. For the past five years they have been struggling with Karl's oppositional and defiant behavior. Oscar felt strongly that his son should do what he was told and be respectful. When Karl didn't do what Oscar told him to do, this "pushed Oscar's buttons," and he would become angry and yell at Karl. I met with Oscar and we had the following discussion.

Therapist: Karl, what do you think makes Oscar act the way he does?
Oscar: He's stubborn and just won't listen.
T: Won't listen?
O: Yeah, I tell him to do something and he won't.
T: I wonder what would make him act that way?
O: I don't know, he's just a stubborn kid.
T: When he acts that way, what do you do?
O: (sheepishly) I yell at him.
T: (in a soft voice) You really get upset when he won't listen.
O: (looks at me) Yes, I do.
T: What's so upsetting for you about this?
O: I just want him to learn to respect authority.
T: Why?
O: Why!?! Because if he's going to do well in life he has to learn to respect those in authority, bosses, teachers, police, all of 'em.
T: (in a surprised voice) Oh, I get it. You become upset because you are afraid your son won't do well in life?
O: Yes, he's a good kid and I want him to do well in life . . . it took me a long time to learn that growing up.
T: Oh, so you are worried Karl will have a hard time, like you did?
O: Yes.
T: Wow, you really love him.
O: Yes.
T: Well, has yelling at him worked so far?
O: I guess if I really think about it, no, it hasn't, but what else can I do? I mean my Dad was a yeller and I eventually learned. Why won't Karl?
T: Yes, you did eventually learn and you also said you had a hard time; it took a long time; is that what you want for Karl?
O: No, not really.
T: OK, so why don't we figure this out and see if we can find another way to help Karl, what do you say?
O: Yes, I'd like that.

understand this, we can then begin to disconnect the button and act therapeutically. Only when the parent has been able to disconnect the button will the parent be able to act therapeutically in the face of various behaviors the child exhibits. The therapist must use tact, sensitivity, and a large dose of empathy to help a parent experience their button and do the exploration necessary to disconnect the button. An important first step is to join with the parent's intentions, which are usually good and then move to how the parent implements those intentions, which may be problematic.

Parents are the key to treatment success. They provide the healing environment within which the child can develop a more secure and healthy pattern of attachment and emotionally meaningful relationships. How the parents create intimacy, safety, security, and a responsive environment is crucial to good outcomes. I describe this as the primacy of parents. As a clinician it is vital that you develop a good working relationship with the parents. Whatever you'd like the parents to do with the child (be responsive, sensitive, and emotionally attuned, be able to create positive concordant intersubjective experiences, be insightful, create a sense of safety) you must be able to do with the parents.

While there are formal methodologies to assess a parent's pattern of attachment, insightfulness, and commitment, if the clinician attends to the process of the interview and the manner in which the parent responds to the clinician, then the clinician can develop some reasonably well-informed hypotheses regarding the parent on each of these dimensions.

ASSESSING STATE OF MIND WITH RESPECT TO ATTACHMENT

The most researched and clinically relevant approach to assessing a person's (age sixteen and above) state of mind with respect to attachment is the Adult Attachment Interview (Hesse, E., 2008; Steele & Steele, 2008). This is a semi-structured interview that takes about an hour to administer and that yields a wealth of clinically significant material. Using this research-based instrument in clinical practice can enrich your understanding of the parents' pattern of attachment, which is very important for your initiating and pacing of treatment. In adults the patterns are: Secure, Preoccupied, Dismissing, and Disorganized. These are categories that have been refined and identified by extensive empirical research across cultures. There is a large body of research supporting these categorizations. In the research literature there are several subtypes within each category and two other categories that we won't be concerned with in this chapter (Earned Secure and Cannot Classify). The Adult Attachment Interview is the primary method for assessing an adult's state of mind with respect to attachment. There is extensive literature regarding this semi-structured interview's reliability and validity. It is a very useful tool for the assessment of adults and is a powerful tool for clinical use. In the Adult Attachment Interview the person's narrative is evaluated along two primary dimensions. The first dimension is coherence. Coherence refers to answers that

- provide a clear and convincing description;
- are truthful, succinct, and complete;
- Are presented in a clear and orderly manner.

The second dimension is the ability to reflect on the motives of others.

In evaluating the adult's narrative we look at four dimensions.

- Quality. To be truthful and to have evidence for what is said.
- Quantity. To be succinct and complete. Make your contribution as informative as is required but no more so.
- Relevance. To be relevant.
- Manner. To be clear and orderly. Avoid obscurity of expression, ambiguity, and be brief and orderly in discourse.

In the general population the percent of people who fall into each pattern is described in table 2.1.

Secure

The adults with a secure pattern of attachment have the capacity to view others with few distortions. They value relationships, emotions, and attachment. When they take the Adult Attachment Interview, their narratives are coherent, collaborative, concise, and comprehensive. They value attachments, and seem objective regarding any particular event or relationship. Descriptions and evaluations of attachment-related experiences are consistent, whether experiences are favorable or unfavorable.

Table 2.1. Adult Patterns of Attachment in the General Population

Pattern	*Range found in research*	*Percentage in Population*
Secure	50-75 percent	60 percent
Avoidant	15-30 percent	20 percent
Ambivalent	5-25 percent	15 percent
Disorganized	5-25 percent	5 percent

Dismissing

Adults with a dismissing pattern of attachment have difficulty viewing others without distortions. As children they learned to not put too many demands on their care-givers in order to get their needs met. These adults are dismissing of attachment-related experiences and relationships. Their narratives tend to be very general and non-specific. They often normalize without specific examples or evidence ("excellent, very normal mother"), with generalized representations of history unsupported or actively contradicted by episodes recounted. Their narratives are much too brief, and violate the criteria of quality. Transcripts also tend to be excessively brief, violating the criteria of quantity.

Preoccupied

Adults with a preoccupied pattern of attachment have difficulty viewing others without distortions. As children they learned that to get their care-givers attention and to get their needs met, they had to be very demanding. Their narratives lack coherence. These adults tend to be preoccupied with or by past attachment relationships and experiences. The speaker often appears angry, passive, or fearful. Sentences are often long, grammatically tangled, and filled with vague usages ("dadada," "and that"), thus violating the criteria of manner and the criteria of relevance. In addition, they tend to ramble on, going off on unrelated tangents and bring in unnecessary details violating the criteria of quantity.

Disorganized

Adults with a disorganized pattern of attachment have difficulty viewing others without significant distortions. As children they had caregivers who were frightening. Often they have experienced chronic early maltreatment within a caregiving relationship and may be described as having significant dysfunction in their capacity to form emotionally meaningful relationships and attachments. During discussions of loss or abuse, these individuals show striking lapses in the monitoring of reasoning or discourse. For example, the individual may briefly indicate a belief that a dead person is still alive in the physical sense, or that this person was killed by a childhood thought. Individual may lapse into prolonged silence or eulogistic speech. Their relationships tend to be volatile.

ASSESSING INSIGHTFULNESS

What is insightfulness? Insightfulness is the ability to reflect on one's experience, the experience of others, and the relationship. It is the capacity to gain an accurate and deep intuitive understanding of a person or relationship. It is derived from the sense of "inner sight," mental vision, or wisdom. It is related to the construct of reflective function (Fonagy, Gergely, Jurist, & Target, 2002).

Why is insightfulness an important parent capacity to be assessed? Quite simply, being responsive, sensitive, and therapeutic require insightfulness. The capacity to objectively and with empathy, reflect on one's own experience, the experience of the other, and the relationship is central to acting therapeutically. Assessing the parent's insightfulness or reflective capacity is essential if the therapist is going to be able to join with and help the parent. Parents with limited or damaged insightfulness and reflective abilities will require more assistance by the therapist to help these parents develop these capacities. This may require extensive time working with the parents without the child to help the parents develop their insightfulness so that they can be most therapeutic with their child.

Self-aware reflection, the reflective function, is a key component of Dyadic Developmental Psychotherapy. It involves "the thinking mind" with regard to the inner world of self and other. This leads to greater understanding and greater flexibility in the responses available. When the parent has a well developed reflective function, this leads to the child experiencing that the child exists in a positive way in the heart and mind of the parent. New meanings lead to new options for action that leads to healthier functioning.

Insightfulness can be formally assessed using the Insightfulness Assessment Procedure (Koren-Karie, N., Oppenheim, D., Dolev S., Sher, E., & Etzion-Carasso, E. 2002; Oppenheim, D., Koren-Karie, N., & Sagi, A. 2001; Oppenheim, D., Goldsmith, D., & Koren-Karie, N. 2005). This procedure can be useful in assessing a parent's insightfulness with children whose ages range from three to approximately ten years old. The procedure involves two steps. First, four parent-child episodes are videotaped. Each episode is about ten or fifteen minutes in length and occurs in a playroom with one parent and the child. The therapist can be observing in the room that contains the videotape equipment. The four episodes are:

- Free play
- Teaching task
- Competition
- Nurturing

The formal questions and methodology for interpreting this procedure will be described below. However, using your clinical judgment, there is a wealth of information you can glean from this procedure. The first episode, Free Play, involves instructing the parent to "play with your child in the room." The play room should have a variety of age-appropriate toys, such as blocks, Lego, doll-house, puppets, dolls and stuffed animals, cars and trucks of various sizes, wooden train set, Lincoln-logs, and so forth. Observing how the parent is able to structure, engage, and maintain the child's focus can provide useful material about the parent-child relationship. The second episode, Teaching Task, involves instructing the parent to "use the Duplo Blocks (large Lego blocks to be set up on a board) to build a shape and have your child build the same exact structure; the same shape, size, and color as the one you are building." Observing how the parent responds to the child—is the parent sensitive to the child's abilities, and does the parent encourages or does not encourage the child—is valuable material. For example, some parent's primary method of "coaching" is to continually inform the child that "that's wrong. . . . No. . . . Not that color. . . . that's not right. . . ." This depicts quite a different relationship than the parent who changes how the parent coaches the child in response to whether the child is building the structure correctly and who offers positive encouragements. The third episode, Competition, involves asking the parent to play "Connect-Four" with the child. This is a relatively quick game so that several episodes can be played in the fifteen minutes. Observing how the parent manages the child's response to winning and losing is instructive. Finally, the last episode, the Nurturing Activity, involves asking the parent to read several stories to the child while sitting on the couch.

The entire tape can be used later to show the parent examples of how the parent was interacting with their child in a way that you would like the parent to do more often. In this manner you are asking the parent to do something that the parent already knows how to do. This builds on the parent's strengths. For example, I was seeing a mother and her six-year-old son because the mother described him as, "never listening and always being defiant." The child had a diagnosis of Attention Deficit/Hyperactivity Disorder and was very active. Throughout the four episodes it was clear that the mother had great difficulty structuring the environment for the child and helping him maintain focus. During the Teaching Activity, at one point, the child began building his own shape and telling his mother how to copy him, which she did. During the Nurturing Activity the child was quite squirmy, hardly looked at the book, and repeatedly asking about different objects in the room. However, at one point his mother reached around her son and then held both sides of the book with a hand while he was in the crook of her arm. At that moment, her son stopped squirming, began looking at the book and was no longer distracted or distracting. I used this small clip to show the mother how her son responded very positively to her gentle and nurturing structuring. This small intervention led to marked changes in their relationship and improvements at home.

Once the tape is made, the therapist then selects a two-minute segment from each episode to be shown to the parent. The specific two-minute segment selected should be the same two-minute segment from each episode (for example, the fourth and fifth minute of each segment).

In a separate session with the parent alone the therapist shows the parent each episode and after viewing the episode, the therapist asks the following three questions.

- What do you think went through your child's mind? What did your child feel and think during this segment?
- Is this segment characteristic of your child more generally? Does it tell you something about your child's personality or characteristics?
- I would now like to ask you about what you felt, while watching this segment. Did anything concern you, surprise you, or make you happy in this segment?

After all four segments are viewed and the parent has responded to the three questions, the parent is asked following set of questions:

- First, from what we talked about during this interview until now, and from what you know about your child in general, what characterizes your child as a person, as a child? What makes <Name of Child><Name of Child>? I will write down what you say and ask you for examples later on.
- Based on how well you know your child, are these things about your child that surprise you, concern you, or make you happy?
- What is the thing that, in your opinion, most characterizes the relationship between your child and yourself?

As you can see, these questions are both simple and have the potential to yield important clinical material. They can provide the therapist with a reasonable assessment of the parent's insightfulness and ability to view the child as a separate individual with different thoughts, feeling, and understandings. In my experience, the greater the parent's insightfulness, the more quickly therapy can progress. Parents lacking insightfulness will require more help and support in order to develop this essential skill.

Assessing Commitment

Parent commitment is the best predictor of placement stability in foster care (Dozier & Lindheim, 2006). In general, parent commitment is a good gauge of how treatment will proceed. The stronger the commitment, all other things being equal, the better the outcome of treatment. Without a strong commitment to the child by the parent, it is likely that the placement will disrupt because the parent will not be willing to tolerate the child's presentations of anxiety, fear, shame, and loss. Children with significant histories of maltreatment often present their shame, fear, anxiety, and feelings of low self-worth in a variety of ways that can be difficult for parents to tolerate, even when the parent is insightful, sensitive, and responsive. Table 2.2 describes some of the common behaviors presented by children with histories of maltreatment and the possible underlying cause.

Table 2.2. Possible Underlying Cause of Behaviors and What Is Needed

Behavior	*Underlying Factors*	*What Is Needed*
"Chronic lies"	Shame. While a toddler may cover his or her eyes or hide, an older child can deny that the child did anything; which is another way of hiding	Acceptance of the underlying feelings; with consequences occurring later.
"Steals"	Lack of trust and being "blind" to the fact that these parents can and will help	Provide what the child needs in a responsive manner.
"Aggressive for no reason"	Fear. Fight-flight-freeze-appeasement is driven by fear; often by some trauma trigger	Increase time with the child to develop more sensitivity so that you can intervene more quickly.

Parent commitment can be evaluated by considering the parent's responses to the nine questions about their child (Dozier & Lindheim, 2006). For example:

1. How much would you miss (child's name) if (child's name) had to leave?
2. How do you think your relationship with (child's name) is affecting (him/her) right now?
3. How do you think your relationship with (child's name) will affect (him/her) in the long-term?

ASSESSING THE CHILD

There are many good texts that describe approaches to assessing children who have Complex Trauma and disorders of detachment. See, for example, A. Becker-Weidman, *Assessing Children with Complex Trauma & Disorders of*

You can roughly gauge the parent's commitment using the following guidelines from Dozzier & Lindheim, 2006.

HIGH

The parent can provide evidence of a strong emotional investment in the child and in parenting the child. Descriptions of the child and the parent-child relationship clearly reflect a strong emotional connection to the child. The child is fully integrated into the family; although the parent may acknowledge that the child will eventually leave the home (e.g., to return to the biological parent in the case of a foster child), the parent considers the child as the parent's while the child is in the home.

MODERATE

The parent provides clear evidence of investment in the child but this is not as strong as with the parent scoring high on commitment. While there may be some indications of a high level of commitment, there may also be evidence suggesting that the child has not been psychologically adopted by the parent. The child may be only partially integrated into the family (the child is placed in respite care when the family goes on vacation, for example). There may also be clear signs of this child being treated differently and less well than the other children in the home.

LOW

The parent provides virtually no evidence of a strong and active emotional investment in the child or in parenting the child. The parent may be indifferent to whether the child remains in the home or may actually state that the parent hopes/desires that the child will be removed. There may be little evidence that the parent would miss the child if the child leaves. The child has not been psychologically adopted by the parent and is not be fully integrated into the family (The child is routinely placed in respite care or does not participate in family activities).

Attachment, DVD set, Resourceful Recordings, Brookfield, VT, 2007, which describes a comprehensive model for the assessment of complex trauma and attachment disorders. In the book *Creating Capacity for Attachment* there is a chapter detailing various elements in the assessment of children (A. Becker-Weidman, "The Logistics of Providing Dyadic Developmental Psychotherapy," in *Creating Capacity for Attachment* (eds., A. Becker-Weidman & D. Shell), pp. 43–56, Wood N Barnes, Oklahoma City, OK, 2005, 2008). Finally, the Association for the Treatment and Training in the Attachment of Children has a professional practices guide with very useful material on assessment and treatment (ATTACh 2009). The most important point here is that any such assessment must be comprehensive and include screening for the various conditions and domains that may be affected by chronic early maltreatment within a care-giving relationship.

Assessing the child can be done either using formal methodologies as described in the texts and DVDs mentioned above, or more informally. What I will outline here is a summary of how I conduct my more formal assessment of a child. This approach is presented for illustration purposes and is not meant to be prescriptive.

I usually meet with the caregivers first and then meet with the child. In my first meeting with the child I usually begin with some innocuous questions such as "What do you want me to call you?" I hold up both my hands and ask the child to point to my left hand. It is interesting how many children with histories of complex trauma who are ten or twelve years old and older point to my right hand. I then use the House-Tree-Person (Buck & Warren, 1995; Wenck, 1997) drawings to engage the child. I first have the child do the drawings in pencil. Later in the interview I will have the child do the drawings in crayon. For many children this is an innocuous task and does not require much talking, although some children find the unstructured instructions, "Please draw a house," anxiety-provoking as they strive to figure out what I want them to do, what is the "right answer." I will ask a few questions about each drawing and then put out the eight crayons from the small Crayola® crayon box for the Heart drawing.

The Heart drawing is something I have developed. I ask the child to pick colors for feelings; "What color would you pick for the feeling mad," then sad, glad, and scared. As the child selects a crayon I ask the child to write that word at the bottom of the page. I then ask the child to draw a large heart on the paper. Next I ask the child to "color in the heart with the amount of each feeling you usually feel most of the time. If you have a lot of one feeling in you put a lot of that color in the heart and if you have only a little bit of a feeling in you put in a little bit, and color in the whole heart." I find that most often children actually do this in a fairly accurate way, reflecting their affective states. Once this drawing is done we can discuss each feeling, what makes the child feel that emotion, what the child does when feeling that emotion, and related questions. Once this is done I will have the child do the House-Tree-Person drawings in crayon. Since color tends to evoke emotions it can be very instructive to compare the pencil drawings with the color drawings.

At this point in the interview I find I can begin to ask other questions about the child's history, relationships, school, peers, and other subjects and that the child has experienced sufficient acceptance, safety, and security in the interview to begin to respond in a more relaxed and open manner. Toward the end of the interview I use the Attachment Story Completion Test (Bretherton & Ridgeway, 1990) to get a sense of the child's state of mind with respect to attachment. The Attachment Story Completion Test is a narrative test in which the therapist reads the beginning of the story and the child then makes up the rest of the story. Each story stem is increasingly "provocative" of attachment related emotions and thinking. The attachment system is essentially a proximity seeking system that is activated when the child experiences some threat. Attachment behavior is proximity seeking behavior. When the child is threatened, the child will seek safety and security with some preferred caregiver. The five story stems are the following:

1. While the family is seated at the dinner table, the younger child accidentally spills juice on the floor, and the mother exclaims about it.
2. While the family is taking a walk in the park, the younger child climbs a rock, falls off, hurts a knee, and cries.
3. After the child is sent upstairs to go to bed, the child cries out after hearing a strange sound.
4. The parents leave for a weekend trip, with grandmother remaining behind to look after the two children.
5. Grandmother looks out of the window on Monday morning and tells the children the parents are coming back.

An important consideration in assessing a child who has a history of chronic early maltreatment within a caregiving relationship is the child's developmental functioning and developmental age; which is often lower than the child's chronological age (Becker-Weidman, 2009). This has a tremendous impact on treatment and parenting. Broadly speaking, we treat people based on their developmental age not chronological age. Since children who have experienced complex trauma and disorders of attachment are functioning at a much younger age than their chronological age, this is quite significant. Knowing the child's developmental level of functioning allows the

COMPONENTS OF A COMPREHENSIVE ASSESSMENT

A comprehensive assessment, in addition to considering the parent factors previously described, should include the following elements.

1. Mental health evaluation and mental status
2. Pattern of attachment
3. Screening for neuro-psychological issues
4. Screening for sensory-integration disorders
5. Screening for prenatal exposure to chemicals
6. Evaluation of major domains:
7. Biology
8. Emotional regulation
9. Behavioral regulation
10. Attachment
11. Cognition
12. Defenses and dissociation
13. Self-concept
14. Academic functioning
15. Social functioning
16. Peer relationships
17. History and placements

therapist to pace treatment accordingly and to advise parents on appropriate parenting approaches.

In conclusion, the first thing for the therapist to be focusing on in Dyadic Developmental Psychotherapy treatment, is building the alliance. A useful phrase for therapists and parents is, "It's about connections, not compliance." The "it" in this statement refers to what is important for parents and therapists to be attending to as they guide and help. Connections are most important. I am not saying that compliance isn't important; that would be far from the truth. Compliance, values, ethics, adherence to rules, and related constructs are important. The question is, "how to get compliance, values, ethics, and adherence to rules?" While is certainly is true that you can get nearly anyone to do nearly anything if you exert enough force; that does not lead to internalization or to following the rules when the person exerting the force is not present. For example, when we put a car thief in jail, that person does not steal anymore cars; at least not while still in jail. But the recidivism rate for car thieves is very high, over 50 percent. What parents want is for their child to internalize their values and beliefs and to "act good," whether or not the parent is present and watching. The way to get compliance is through connections.

It is through a relationship that the child begins to internalize the parent's values, beliefs, and ethics. A strong connection (or a healthy and secure pattern of attachment) can lead to the child internalizing the parent's values, beliefs, and ethics. A strong connection can lead to the child *wanting* to please the parent, and compliance then follows. The child who has a strong positive connection and relationship with the parent wants to please the parent and feels good when the parent is happy with the child and the child's behavior; this will lead to compliance.

A parent described the following story to me that exemplifies what I am describing. This family would use as a consequence the removal of "screens" (CRTs, TV, videos, games, cell phone, computer, etc.) whenever their son misbehaved. When their twenty-two-year-old son, who by now was three inches taller and forty pounds larger than his father, was home from college one summer he did something that the father was not pleased with, so the father said to his son, "That's it, no screens for the weekend." The young man looked at his father and said, "Can you do that?" to which the father replied, "Yes, I'm your father." The parent described how for about half a minute he could see his son thinking something like, "Oh, bummer, it's gonna be a boring week; and I had plans too." The father then realized that this wasn't the best approach and he and his son had a chat about what the father was unhappy with and that was the end of that. However, the parent was struck with how his son seemed willing to accept the "punishment." So, I am not saying, "don't expect compliance." What I am saying is that it is through building a relationship, through connections, that real compliance is achieved.

We can now move on to the next chapter, which is about a trauma and attachment perspective. This perspective provides a new lens to understand the child and the family and is central to the practice of Dyadic Developmental Psychotherapy. The assessments described in this chapter can provide the basis for beginning work as a practitioner of Dyadic Developmental Psychotherapy.

Chapter 3

A Trauma and Attachment Perspective

This chapter describes the theoretical framework for therapy, the perspective that the therapist practicing Dyadic Developmental Psychotherapy uses in work with parents, children, and families. The basic framework is attachment theory as developed by John Bowlby. There are many excellent texts about attachment theory and about attachment theory as applied to Dyadic Developmental Psychotherapy (Becker-Weidman & Shell 2005/2008). This chapter will focus on several implications of attachment theory for treatment and on a few related concepts that can be integrated into the practice of Dyadic Developmental Psychotherapy.

The first important implication of attachment theory as applied by Dyadic Developmental Psychotherapy is that the focus must be on causes and not symptoms. The therapist continually strives to "go deeper" with the family in order to focus on the drivers of behavior. It is the emotions underlying behavior that are the primary focus. A simple behavior can have multiple causes and it is the cause that is treated; otherwise the therapist and family end up playing a game of "Wack-A-Mole" (that arcade game in which the moles keep popping up faster and faster).

CAUSES MATTER

Consider Mary, who has attention problems. Mary's parents describe her as a child who cannot focus, cannot pay attention in class, has difficulty doing what they ask her to do, is sloppy in work, is easily distracted and led off-task, is hyper-active, and is always moving. The parents are increasingly annoyed with Mary's seeming unwillingness to cooperate with the family and to do her chores. She leaves her jacket on the floor, forgets her homework, and constantly loses nice things like gloves and hats. Certainly these are behaviors seen in children with Attention Deficit/Hyperactivity Disorder. These are also behaviors seen in children with sensory-integration dysfunction, traumatic brain injury, Alcohol Related Neurological Dysfunction, and Complex Trauma. Each of these conditions is treated differently. Understanding Mary makes a huge difference in how her parents will feel about her, and how her parents feel will make a huge difference in how they act toward her and, in turn, how Mary responds to them. Mary's parents viewed her disorganization, losing things, and non-compliance as willful acts purposely done to annoy them. They said that a nine-year-old should be able to do better. What is the approach of Dyadic Developmental Psychotherapy? No lectures is one important caveat. The first step, of course, would be a thorough assessment to determine what may be going on with Mary emotionally, psychologically, and developmentally. A better understanding of what is "driving" Mary's behaviors, allows a productive discussion, similar to the following, with her parents. Notice that in this example I do not begin with a lecture. I begin by asking questions to explore their understanding of Mary, accepting their view and then being curious about their view. This allows me to develop empathy for the parents and help them see their daughter in a different light.

The following dialogue occurred at the end of the meeting with the parents in which I reviewed the results of a comprehensive assessment of their daughter.

Therapist: So, what do you think leads Mary to act the way she does?
Mr. Thomas: Well, I think she likes making us angry.
T: What would make her do that?
Mr.: I don't know; maybe she enjoys seeing me upset. Martha, what do you think?
Mrs. Thomas: I don't know Henry. She really can be so annoying, but she's such a sweet girl. It's confusing.
Mr.: I know what you mean. I take her out, and we have a nice day, and I buy her a new hat for winter, and then she leaves it on the bench. What's wrong with her?
T: Let me ask you something. If you think of your daughter's behavior, at what age would you consider her behavior "normal?"
Mrs.: Oh, when you put it that way, I'd have to say about three. Henry?
Mr.: Yes, three sounds right, but she's not three; she's almost ten!
T: But she often acts like she's three?
Mr.: Well, yes, I guess.

T: So, if she were three, would you have done anything differently about the hat?
Mr.: Sure, I'd have let her wear it, and when she took it off on the bench to eat, I'd have put it in her pocket.
T: If you'd done that, what would have happened?
Mr.: Well, she'd not have left it on the bench, and I guess I'd not be angry at her for being so careless; three-year-olds aren't careless; they're just being three. But she's ten for God's sake.
T: She was six when she moved in?
Mrs.: Yes, she'd been in the orphanage in Siberia most of that time. She was only with her birth family for about a year and a half before the authorities took her because the parents were alcoholic and neglecting her.
T: So, she probably was prenatally exposed to alcohol?
Mrs.: Maybe; we really don't know much about her early years.
T: But it's possible, and her profile on the Behavior Rating Inventory of Executive Function as completed by both you and her teacher does show significant impairments in areas like working memory, emotional control, and several other executive functions consistent with neuropsychological dysfunction related to alcohol exposure.
Mr. & Mrs.: Yes.
T: So, what might make Mary act the way she does?
Mrs.: The orphanage life was pretty bad there; lots of children and only a few caretakers. I know she was often hungry and really didn't have anyone to take care of her. She only seemed to miss the other children. And if her birth mother drank, that can cause problems, can't it?
T: So, what you are saying is that maybe we have a child who is, at times, developmentally younger than her chronological age, perhaps because of early pervasive neglect, who also has some cognitive difficulties, perhaps caused by prenatal exposure to alcohol. Could that be?
Mr.: That makes a lot of sense. Oh, I feel terrible. How could I have yelled at her all those times?!
Mrs.: (crying) Oh my God; have we made things worse?
T: You both feel badly about not knowing what was going on with your daughter?
Mr. & Mrs.: Yes.
Mrs.: What do we do now?
T: It seems that now you have a more helpful understanding of what makes Mary act the way she does and can now help her better because of your new understanding.
Mr.: So, she probably needs a lot more supervision and help from us?

So, as you can see, in this very brief example, developing a fuller understanding of what is causing the child to act as she does can lead to the parents feeling quite differently and then acting in a more helpful manner.

AN ATTACHMENT PERSPECTIVE

An attachment perspective leads the therapist to think in terms of an alliance, a secure base, relationships, exploration, joyful interactions, and reciprocal interactions. A phrase that we will come back to throughout this book, since it captures many of the core principles of Dyadic Developmental Psychotherapy and outlines the phases and process of treatment, is the following:

> Creating an **ALLIANCE** is necessary to create a SECURE BASE. The **SECURE BASE** is necessary to begin EXPLORATION. **EXPLORATION** is necessary to achieve INTEGRATION. **INTEGRATION** is necessary to achieve **HEALING.**

It all begins with creating an alliance with the parents, family, and child. An alliance with the parents, the creation of a secure base, is necessary so that the parents feel safe in therapy. This secure base with the parents allows the therapist to begin exploring other ways of viewing the family and other ways of parenting. Ultimately, this will lead to helping heal the child. Dyadic Developmental Psychotherapy relies heavily on building and maintaining an emotionally meaningful relationship as a central "active ingredient" in being therapeutic and healing. It is these experiences that lead to healing.

Treatment, the building and maintaining of the alliance and the creation of the secure base from which exploration can occur begins with the parents. Whatever is expected of parent-child interaction, the therapist has to be able to do and create with the parents. As a secure base is created for the parents in treatment, the parents can begin to create a healing environment in the home and the real work of healing can begin.

A TRAUMA PERSPECTIVE

Attachment Theory and Trauma Theory fit together well. In fact, the very definition of Complex Trauma (Cook et. al. 2003; Cook et. al. 2005) is rooted in attachment terms. Complex Trauma can be defined as having four elements. Complex Trauma is

1. Chronic
2. Early
3. Maltreatment within a
4. Caregiving relationship

Complex Trauma can result in impairment in seven domains of functioning, which are:

1. Attachment
2. Behavioral regulation
3. Emotional regulation
4. Cognition
5. Defenses (dissociation, primarily)
6. Biology
7. Self-concept

Naturally, a thorough assessment must consider to what extent there is impairment in each of these domains so that treatment interventions are tailored to account for these difficulties.

A trauma perspective, as integrated into the practice of Dyadic Developmental Psychotherapy, involves two important principles. The first is Safety First. Without physical, psychological, and emotional safety, the difficult work of exploring the past and integrating the trauma cannot occur. This principle from trauma treatment refers to the attachment theory principle of building an alliance in order to create a secure base from which exploration can occur. The second principle of trauma treatment is that one must revisit the trauma in a titrated manner to avoid dysregulation; Briere & Scott (2006) refer to this as maintaining the "therapeutic window." This concept means that in order for healing to occur the client must be experiencing some affect (above the window sill), but not so much that the person becomes dysregulated. This is affect regulation, and the co-regulation of emotions within a therapeutic relationship is an important component of Dyadic Developmental Psychotherapy. As will be described later, the creation of positive concordant intersubjective experiences is one element of affect regulation and a component of Dyadic Developmental Psychotherapy.

Effects of Complex Trauma on Development and Functioning

Developmental Delays

One of the profound effects of chronic early maltreatment within a caregiving relationship on development is significant developmental delays. Children who have experienced complex trauma often function at a developmental age that is significantly lower than their chronological age (Becker-Weidman, 2009). These developmental delays in the domains of communications (expressive and receptive), daily living skills, socialization, and motor skills in the case of younger children, can create a variety of difficulties that the therapist must carefully address. Peer relationships are negatively affected by these delays and become increasingly problematic as the child ages. These

Sarah and Mark were concerned that Josh, age nine, was, in their words, "constantly disobedient."

Sarah: He never does what I ask him to do.
Therapist: Can you give me an example?
Mark: Sure, this morning, after I woke him up for school, I told him to go into the bathroom, get washed, brush his teeth, get dressed and come downstairs for breakfast. Twenty minutes later he's still standing in the bathroom, water is all over the place, he's not dressed or washed, and now he's gonna be late for school, and I'm gonna be late for work!
Sarah: Sometimes I think he's just acting stupid to make me mad.
Therapist: Has he always been like that?
Sarah: Since we got him three years ago, yes.
T: What would make him act that way?
M: I don't know; that's why we're here.
T: Well, I mean, you know Josh better than I do, and you've probably puzzled over his behavior for a while now. What "theories" have you come up with to explain what he does? (Note: This sort of question can be a useful informal way of beginning to assess the parent's insightfulness.)
S: Like I said, I think he just likes to make us mad; I think he thinks it's fun.
T: What an odd thing to do; what would make him want to get you two angry at him? (In Dyadic Developmental Psychotherapy terms, I accept their view and then ask questions to better understand (empathy) their view.)
S: It is strange because when I do get mad at him, he seems really upset.
M: That's right. He acts like he can't do these things, but he's nine years old!
T: Let me ask you this, at what age would Josh have to be for you to say, "Well, any child that age would act that way?"
M: Well, now that you mention it, he does sort of act a lot like Dana, our twelve-year-old, did when Dana was three and four.
S: Yes, that's true. Sometimes I think he never really grew up; he was removed from his birth parents when he was four because they neglected and abused him, and he was in several foster homes before he came to us three years ago.
T: So, if he actually was three or four, you'd not have any concerns about his behavior?
M: Not really.
S: No, I'd never send a four-year-old into the bathroom and expect him to get washed and dressed all by himself.

T: Well, maybe Josh, in some ways, is still a four-year-old and needs your help to catch up to his chronological age. What do you think would happen, Mark, if each morning you woke him up, took him into the bathroom, washed him up, brushed his teeth, and got him dressed?
M: I bet he'd love it. But how will he ever learn to do these things if I keep doing them for him?
T: Did Dana ever learn?
M: Well, yes.
T: And how did that happen?
M: Well, we just helped him along.
S: Remember how we'd brush his teeth and then one day he grabbed the brush from your hand, Mark, and said, "Me do it!!" and how you smiled and we were so proud of him.
M: So what you're saying is that if we meet him where he is he'll eventually grow up?
T: It worked with Dana didn't it?
M: Yes.
T: I think if you meet Josh where he is developmentally, and do these things for him, then with him, and make it fun, that the normal developmental processes will move him along and he'll eventually do these things all on his own.

developmental delays also can be compounded when the family expects the child to "act" the child's chronological age and the child is not able to do so. In those instances, the child can become increasingly frustrated by being expected to act in ways that the child cannot; this only further increases the child's frustration and dysregulation, further upsetting the parents. The parents may become increasingly frustrated that their child is seemingly oppositional and defiant. These negative attributions, based on the assumption that the child is capable of doing what has been asked and "non-compliance" is experienced as defiance, oppositional behavior, or as controlling. This further erodes the parent-child relationship and creates a downward spiral of increasing dysregulation and parental frustration and annoyance. The Dyadic Developmental Psychotherapist's responsibility is to accurately assess the child's developmental functioning and age and then to help the parents experience their child in a new way.

In a study (Becker-Weidman, 2009) of the developmental age of children with complex trauma, it was found that they had an age equivalent score of 4.6 years in personal care while averaging nearly ten years old, chronologically. Therefore, it is not unusual for these children to have poor hygiene. Expecting such a child to be able to properly wash or brush teeth often leads to frequent battles between parent and child. The parents often feel frustrated with what they perceive as the child's lack of compliance, and the child may feel frustrated by being asked to do something which is beyond the child's ability at that time. Having the parent engage in the task with the child, making it an enjoyable, mutually shared experience, can be therapeutic by reducing conflict and stress and by improving the quality of the parent-child relationship. The shift from "compliance" to "teaching/helping" can have a very positive effect on the relationship and the child's functioning.

Neurodevelopment

Chronic early maltreatment within a caregiving relationship can cause significant cognitive impairments and neuro-psychological dysfunction (Mattson, 2010). These difficulties can make it difficult for children to learn and retain new information both at home and in school. A child may learn the seven-times tables today and then have no recollection of that the next day. It may appear to the parent that the child is giving the parent a hard time, but, in fact, it may be that the information did not make it from short-term into long-term memory. If a parent assumes the child knows the seven-times tables and is only being "difficult," the parent will feel annoyed and act according; this may only increase the child's frustration and fear and increase the child's dysregulation. Understanding the nature and extent of any neuropsychological dysfunction can help parents and teachers reframe and understand the child's behavior, going a long way to reducing dysregulation.

Dyadic Developmental Psychotherapy relies on a variety of well-founded elements of treatment such as affect arousal and regulation, gradual exposure to trauma and parent education and consultation. All of these elements of treatment aid in explaining how the past may be continuing to influence present behavior. Forming and maintaining a therapeutic relationship through therapist acceptance, affirmation, empathy, and various other dimensions (Lambert, 2004), are core principles of Dyadic Developmental Psychotherapy.

The Learning and Survival Brains

Chronic early maltreatment within a caregiving relationship affects the brain and behavior. In simple terms there are two functional brain states, the survival brain and the learning brain. Each is good at what it does.

The survival brain comes into play when the person is threatened. The survival brain focuses attention, behavior, and emotions into cognitive and behavioral activities that are more likely to increase the chances of survival. Fight-flight-freeze-appeasement is one example of the survival brain's activities. When faced with threat, a person reacts behaviorally and without the leadership of the cerebral cortex with one of those four strategies. When the survival brain is active, the cerebral cortex is largely inactive or disconnected. Higher brain functions such as planning, evaluation, and other executive functions are largely non-functional when the survival brain is functioning. For this reason, being in the survival brain state is not conducive to learning new information.

The learning brain is functioning when a person is feeling largely safe, secure, and comfortable. The learning brain functions best when a person has a secure base from which to explore. The learning brain is focused on acquiring new information and integrating that into the person's current internal working models and memories. The learning brain uses the cerebral cortex and the various executive functions associated with the cortex. The learning brain is flexible, curious, and open to new experiences.

Children who have experienced complex trauma spend a large amount of time with their survival brain operating. This was an adaptive response to living in an environment of chronic maltreatment. In such a home, the child is under near continual threat, and so the survival brain has primacy. It should not be surprising that such children may have a variety of learning problems, memory difficulties, and dysregulation. The therapist can help parents see how the survival brain inhibits learning by their child and reframe much of what the child does or does not do as rooted in the effects of having the survival brain functioning much of the time.

Implications of a Trauma-Attachment Perspective

A trauma-attachment perspective leads to an understanding that all behavior is adaptive or was adaptive at some time in the past. What often creates difficulties for families is that while the child is no longer in the maltreating home, the child functions as if the child still were in that home. The survival brain makes it difficult for new experiences to take hold, and so the old experiences and patterns continue to emerge. Ingrained patterns of behavior, emotions, and relating continue to operate in the new home. Relating past maltreatment to current difficulties can help reframe the behavior; it once was helpful but now is not. This can help parents reframe their child's behavior and have positive or kind attributions rather than negative attributions regarding the child's motives and intentions.

Another treatment implication of having a trauma-attachment perspective is that many of the symptoms of trauma, such as flashbacks and dissociation, are now viewed as adaptive responses to what were overwhelming experiences. The mind is wonderfully adaptive and has what might be called natural or innate coping mechanisms. One such mechanism for coping with a traumatic event is to "reprocess" it; repeat it and recall it over and over until the impact is diminished. Everyone has experienced some fright, such as a near accident on the highway. What most people do is tell someone—a friend at work, a partner, or a colleague. The story is repeated several times, and by the end of the day the event has receded into the background and no longer has the emotional import it previously had. This repetition is one of the mind's methods of coping with trauma. If an event is overwhelming, one may experience "depersonalization" or dissociation. In these instances the mind copes with overwhelming trauma and events by splitting off the emotional components of the event from the "episodic" elements. The event is experienced "as if watching a movie." Later, the emotions may come flooding back. If the event is extremely traumatic, the episodic elements of memory of the event and the emotional components may remain partially dissociated from each other. In that instance, triggers such as sights, sounds, or smells may trigger the emotional components of the dissociated memory, and the person experiences a "flashback," a reliving of the event rather than a remembering of the event. It is not that the person is here and recalling what happened "there and then." Rather, the person is experiencing the dissociated emotions and reliving the event as if it is happening here and now. These ways that the mind copes with trauma and heals itself are the basis for the principle that the trauma must be revisited, but in a titrated manner, so that the client is kept within the therapeutic window. The Dyadic Developmental Psychotherapist's task is to maintain a healing PACE of treatment, evoking affect, but not causing dysregulation, to achieve integration of the dissociated affect with the episodic memories. Co-regulation of affect by engaging the client in concordant intersubjectivity and PACE are the components, among others, that the therapist will rely on. This is a primary objective during the integration phase of treatment, which will be described in detail later in this book.

There are several other implications of an attachment-trauma perspective for treatment that are central to the practice of Dyadic Developmental Psychotherapy. These include the importance of creating concordant intersubjective experiences; that experiences, more than words, are healing; and that treatment must be relational.

Intersubjectivity refers to shared emotion, attention, and intention. It emerges from shared emotion, which is also called attunement, joint attention and awareness, and congruent intentions. When all three dimensions are in sync, there is concordant intersubjectivity. If one or more of these dimensions are out of sync, there is discordant intersubjectivity. For example, children experience themselves as being delightful, loveable, and clever whenever their caregivers experience them as manifesting those characteristics. In a similar way, the parents experience themselves as being capable and caring whenever their children experience them as manifesting those traits. It is

INTERSUBJECTIVITY

In this example, the therapist helps the parent use the concept of intersubjectivity to make sense of the child's behavior and repair the relationship.

Emma: Last night Beth and I were playing a board game and I thought we were having a fun time, but all of a sudden Beth threw over the board, burst into tears and stormed out of the room screaming, "I hate you and I'm not stupid!"
Therapist: Let's figure out what happened.
E: OK
T: So, you both were playing a game, right?
E: Yes, we were both really into it.
T: OK, so you both had all your attention focused on the game and were enjoying each other and the game? (Here we see shared attention and share emotion)
E: I thought so until she had that bizarre tantrum.
T: What were you trying to do? What was your intention?
E: Me? I just wanted to have fun with Beth. I enjoy being with her, and I just wanted to do something together that we'd both enjoy.
T: Right before Beth's tantrum, what happened in the game?
E: We were playing Uno, and I'd just called UNO and was gonna win.
T: What do you think Beth was trying to do? What was her intention?
E: Oh, now I see. Beth was trying to win and now that I think about it, she says she feels stupid because she doesn't seem to know what many of the other children in her class know. She's still struggling learning English.
T: So maybe you were playing the game to have fun with Beth, and Beth's intention was to win and for her she felt winning or losing reflected on how smart she is?
E: Yes, that makes sense. It's like we were playing two different games together. I was playing to enjoy being with my daughter and I just happened to be winning. Beth was playing to win so that she'd feel smart or not stupid. I guess we should probably play games that don't involve winning or losing, or maybe we should talk about winning and losing before we play and how she'll feel if she wins or loses.

extremely difficult to experience the self as possessing these features if the important people in our lives do not experience us as having these traits.

It is the nature and quality of the experiences we create in therapy that in many respects is more important than words. Experiences are multi-channeled. Experiences can include words. Experiences also include emotions and may include movement, tone of voice, volume, cadence, gestures, and other dimensions. Experiences have a depth that makes them more powerful than mere words alone.

Treatment for disorders of attachment and trauma must be relational since the nature of these difficulties is and was relational. Dyadic Developmental Psychotherapy is primarily a relationship-based treatment. It uses relationship experiences as the primary mechanism for healing. The principle is that the creation of new and therapeutic relationship experiences will help repair the damage created by traumatic and destructive relationships. Since the damage and difficulties the child or parent is experiencing are primarily relational in nature, the treatment must also be relational in nature.

This chapter described the trauma and attachment perspective that is at the heart of Dyadic Developmental Psychotherapy. This perspective leads to some very specific implications for treatment. Dyadic Developmental Psychotherapy has as its core, or central therapeutic mechanism for treatment success, the maintenance of a contingent, collaborative, sensitive, reflective, and affectively attuned relationship between therapist and child, between caregiver and child, and between therapist and caregiver. Dyadic Developmental Psychotherapy focuses on and relies upon the intersubjective sharing and joint development and organization of emotional experiences.

Chapter 4

Components of Dyadic Developmental Psychotherapy

This chapter describes fourteen components of Dyadic Developmental Psychotherapy. I have taken many of Dan Hughes' ideas and reorganized them into a different format and added several constructs that reflect my thinking about treatment. The mix of components is largely determined by the immediate experience in the session, which is a function of the phase of treatment, which will be described in the next chapter. For example, in the first phase of treatment, Developing an Alliance, managing intersubjectivity, follow-lead-follow, and interactive repair are major components while coherent narrative may play a much smaller role.

The basic principles of Dyadic Developmental Psychotherapy may be summarized in the following four paragraphs.

1. Both the caregivers' and therapist's own attachment strategies are organized and resolved before the onset of the child's treatment. Previous research (Tyrell et al. 1999; Dozier et al. 2001) has shown the importance of the caregivers' and therapist's state of mind with respect to attachment for good treatment outcomes.

2. The therapist and caregiver provide the intersubjective experiences for the child that were seldom present in situations of abuse and neglect. These intersubjective experiences are characterized by shared emotion (affect), attunement, shared awareness and attention, and complementary intentions. In addition, these intersubjective experiences should be both concordant and positive. Intersubjective experiences are the primary means by which the infant and young child learn about self, other, and the world (Trevarthen 2001). Intrafamilial trauma and complex trauma will significantly disrupt the development of concordant intersubjectivity and increase the risk that the child will be unable to create a coherent meaning for many events,

particularly traumatic ones. The therapist must provide concordant intersubjective experiences for the parent that help create a secure base within which the parent, child, and therapist can co-create new and more therapeutic meanings for experiences.

Whenever possible, the child's primary caregiver (biological, adoptive, or foster parent or primary caregiver in a residential setting) is an active participant in the session. The therapist must provide to the caregiver support and guidance in communicating thoughts, emotions, and intentions to the child. The primary caregiver serves as the primary source of safety, security, and comfort while the child explores events, experiences, and emotions that may generate fear and shame. The caregiver's presence allows the therapist to facilitate the successful exploration and resolution of behavior problems in the home by modeling for the parent PACE (Playful, Accepting, Curious, Empathic, described more fully below) as an effective means of achieving conflict resolution and increasing emotional and behavioral regulation within the home. The therapist will generally only see a child, usually a teenager, as an individual client when a primary attachment figure is not available. In these instances, the treatment will proceed at a markedly slower pace since the child is essentially emotionally alone the rest of the week in the process of integrating the therapeutic themes. The lack of a primary attachment figure is a severe impediment to creating the security and safety necessary for exploration and integration.

3. Use of PACE and PLACE. These acronyms describe the "attitude" of the therapist and caregiver. PACE refers to the therapist setting a healing pace of treatment by being playful, accepting, curious and empathic. Through PACE, the therapist is able to both generate and regulate the emerging emotions that are associated with the events being explored. Positive concordant intersubjective experiences are largely created with PACE. The therapist is also able to facilitate an open, reflective attitude to reorganize the experience of these events through the therapist's accepting and curious stance. PLACE refers to the parent creating a healing place or environment by being playful, loving, accepting, curious and empathic. All interventions are utilized within the context of PACE along with the other principles presented in this chapter. Any technique may lead to dysregulation if these basic principles, which are needed to generate general safety, are ignored. These ideas are described in more detail in Becker-Weidman & Shell (2005/2008), Becker-Weidman & Shell (2010), and Hughes (2006, 2007, in press).

4. The inevitable misattunements and conflicts that arise in relationships are directly addressed and repaired through the ongoing qualities of the relationship using PACE. The creation of concordant intersubjectivity facilitates the co-creation of meaning and the co-regulation of emotions. The need for

interactive repair is especially important as the themes being explored are often characterized by shame and fear. Repair helps with both affect and behavioral regulation. Repair directly addresses the child's convictions, based on past negative experiences of neglect and abuse, that the child must face stressful events alone or that any conflict will lead to abandonment. The attachment figures are responsible for the initiation of repair, not the child. These same principles apply to the therapist-caregiver relationship. Inevitable misattunements between therapist and parent are directly addressed and repaired thought the relationship. It is the therapist's responsibility to initiate the repair, not the parent.

MAIN COMPONENTS OF DYADIC DEVELOPMENTAL PSYCHOTHERAPY

- Therapist use of self
- Process focused: It's about connections not compliance
- PLACE and PACE
- Intersubjectivity
- Reflective Capacity
- Affective/Reflective dialogue
- Commitment
- Insightfulness
- Coherent narrative
- Co-regulation of emotions
- Co-creation of meanings
- Follow-lead-follow
- Interactive repair
- Nonverbal-verbal dialogue

THERAPIST USE OF SELF

A carpenter uses levels, saws, nails, and hammers. An auto mechanic uses wrenches, gauges, and monitors. The Dyadic Developmental Psychotherapist uses self. Use of self by the therapist is at the core of how Dyadic Developmental Psychotherapy is implemented. Use of self involves the creation and maintenance of concordant intersubjective experiences, the sharing of one's experiences of the other in a therapeutic manner. This use of self is always focused on helping the client achieve greater self knowledge, more flexible modes of relating, and more authentic emotional experiences that reflect the nature and quality of the current relationship. All the other components of Dyadic Developmental Psychotherapy are enacted through the therapist's use of self. It is through the use of self that positive concordant intersubjective experiences can be created and maintained. PACE is largely a function of the therapist's use of self in a therapeutic manner. The therapeutic use of self requires a fairly well developed reflective function and secure state of mind with respect to attachment. As the therapist creates concordant intersubjective experiences, the therapist monitors the effect on the other and the other's emotional experience. The goal is to create emotionally meaningful experiences that facilitate the integration of memories and emotions that were dissociated (split off) as the result of early relational trauma. The therapist must constantly monitor the other's affective state to keep the interactions emotionally meaningful and not dysregulating. The therapist must also monitor the experience so that the dialogue does not become exclusively a cognitive intellectualized dialogue devoid of emotion. The therapist's use of self involves keeping up an affective/reflective dialogue among family members. By reflecting on and monitoring the immediately occurring experiences, the therapist keeps a balance between the affective and the reflective elements of the dialogue. The therapeutic use of self as described here is what allows for the creation of a new and coherent autobiographical narrative, the co-regulation of emotions, and the co-creation of new meanings. Much of this occurs on a non-verbal level through the use of tone of voice, volume, gestures, cadence, expressions, and modulation of voice: the verbal–non-verbal dialogue. In order to help the client explore potentially painful and disturbing memories, emotions, and experiences, the therapist consciously follows the client (through acceptance and curiosity), then leads the client deeper, and again follows at this deeper level. Finally, when inevitable misunderstandings arise, the therapist must be able to manage the experience of shame so that the therapist can accept responsibility for the therapist's mistake. By acknowledging one's errors, mistakes, and misjudgments, the first steps toward interactive repair can occur.

To effectively and therapeutically use self, the therapist must have a relatively secure state of mind with respect to attachment, reasonably developed reflective abilities, good self-awareness, and be tolerant of ambiguity. A secure state of mind with respect to attachment has been found to be important in therapeutic work (Tyrell, et. al., 1999). A secure state of mind with respect to attachment allows the therapist to experience a range of emotions and to reflect on these emotions in a relatively unbiased manner. Self-knowledge involves being aware of personal biases and being able to reflect on internal states. The therapist must be aware of to what extent what experiences reflect the current interactions with the other and to what extent the experiences reflect personal past history being evoked by the current interactions. Finally, tolerance for ambiguity is an important element for use of self because being tolerant of ambiguity allows the therapist not to jump prematurely to conclusions regarding what the other is experiencing and the meaning the other ascribes to the experiences. This suspension of certainty allows the therapist to form various hypotheses regarding the meaning of experiences while keeping an open mind, so that the therapist's curiosity can emerge in an authentic and emotionally meaningful manner. Uncertainty promotes curiosity and questions with an emotional tone that reflect genuine interest in and acceptance of the other's thoughts, feelings, meanings, and experiences.

Therapist use of self is the hub around which all the other elements of Dyadic Developmental Psychotherapy act as spokes, creating the therapeutic and healing experiences that form the outer rim.

THERAPIST USE OF SELF

- Reflective Capacity
- Insightfulness
- Commitment
- Coherent Narrative
- Co-regulation of Emotions
- Co-creation of Meanings
- Follow-Lead-Follow
- Interactive Repair
- Verbal-Non-verbal Dialogue
- Intersubjectivity
- PACE & PLACE
- Affective-Reflective Dialogue
- Connections not Compliance

IT'S ABOUT CONNECTIONS NOT COMPLIANCE

Relationships (friendly, intimate, therapeutic, etc) are built on connections or experiences that have emotional valance and value. The Dyadic Developmental Psychotherapy therapist focuses primarily on relationships and connections, not compliance. It is not that compliance is not important; it is. It is that the way to secure genuine and authentic compliance is through connections and relationships. The use of sufficient force may make a person do almost anything, but remove the force, and the person may not comply. Put a car thief in jail, and no more car thefts, or at least not till the person is back on the streets. What parents are expecting is not necessarily compliance when the parent is watching. What parents usually intend is compliance because it feels right to the child. Ideally, the child does what the child is expected to do, not because the child fears the parent or fears punishment, but because the child feels good when "doing good" and feels bad when "doing bad." When therapists are helping parents help their child, one of the problems they frequently hear is, "He just won't do what I tell him." Parents may try reasoning, yelling, punishing, and all sorts of behavioral methods to secure compliance, often without any long term effectiveness. The way to secure acceptance and adherence is by developing a relationship with emotional valance and depth. Such a relationship is build in numerous experiences of positive concordant intersubjectivity, within which the child feels understood, accepted, and loved. When there is an emotionally meaningful tie between parent and child, the child will value the parent's approval, and over time that good feeling is internalized so that the child feels good when "doing good" and feels bad when "doing bad." The child, developmentally speaking, has moved from shame (which is about who the child is) to guilt (which is about what the child does). Shame causes the person to want to hide or deny what happened because it is about the person. Guilt is about what the person did and leads to wanting to confess and fix the damage.

PACE & PLACE

PACE is the attitude of the therapist. It is the therapist's responsibility to maintain a healing pace of treatment. It is an acronym for being Playful, Accepting, Curious, and Empathic. PLACE is the attitude of the caregiver. It is the caregiver's responsibility to maintain a healing place. It is an acronym for being Playful, Loving, Accepting, Curious, and Empathic. It forms the core of how the therapist or parent begins to explore an event or issue. PACE is also the primary means of initiating "interactive repair" (described below) during the session. This is required whenever the child initiates a break in the relationship or the break is created by a misattuned initiative or response by the therapist or parent.

Figure 4.1 shows this process.

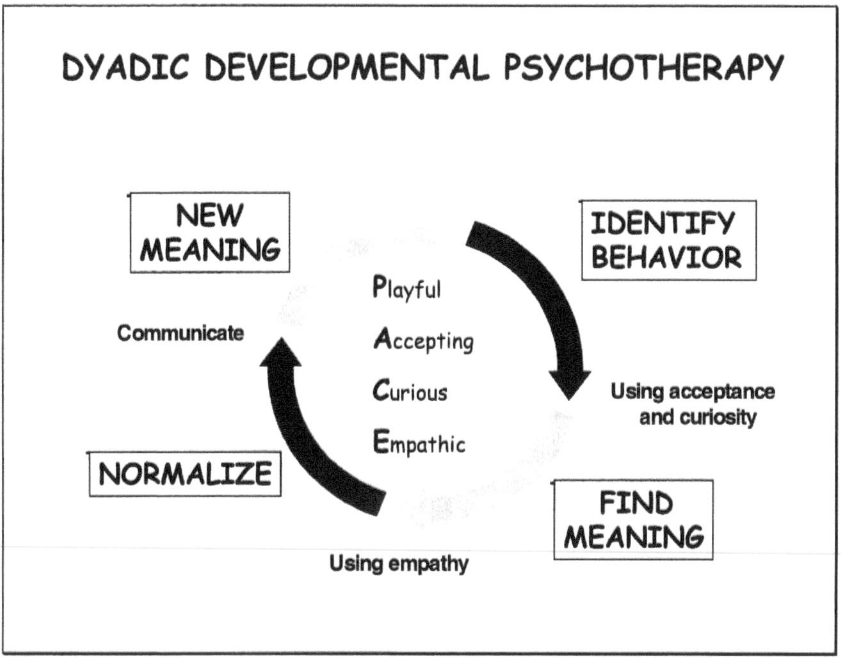

First, behavior is identified and explored. The behavior may have occurred just now or have occurred at some time in the past. Second, using curiosity and acceptance as the behavior is explored, the meaning to the child begins to emerge. Third, empathy is used to reduce the child's sense of shame and increase the child's sense of being accepted and understood. Fourth, the child's behavior is then normalized. In other words, once the meaning of the behavior and its basis in past trauma is identified, it becomes understandable that the behavior is present. Fifth, the child and caregiver communicate this understanding with each other. Sixth, finally, a new meaning for the behavior is found, and the child's actions are integrated into a coherent autobiographical narrative by communicating the new experience and meaning with the caregiver.

An example of such an interaction may illustrate this process more clearly. Sarah, age nine, comes in with her foster mother, Mary. In a meeting with the therapist before the joint session, Mary reports that "out of the blue" Sarah attacked her in the living room while they were cleaning up. Mary is upset and says, "I'm not sure if I can keep a child in my home like Sarah who is so randomly and unpredictably aggressive." The joint session begins with Sarah, Mary, and the therapist.

T: Hi Sarah. How are you?
S: I was bad (said in a soft voice with head down and eyes on her knees. Sarah is probably feeling shame. Notice her use of words. She says "I was bad," not "I did something bad." This is NOT your cue to give Sarah the lecture "Now, you know, Sarah, YOU are not BAD, just sometimes you do bad things." Instead, I accept Sarah's view and explore it with curiosity to understand what it means to Sarah. I want to enter her experience with her.)
T: What happened?
S: Well, I hit and kicked Mom yesterday evening.
T: Well, what happened? (Notice, I do not ask "Why did you do that?" Probably Sarah does not know why she did it. Together we will discover "why.")
S: We were cleaning up the living room, and I knew she was mad at me. (Looking at her foster mother through the hair covering her eyes.)

Note: Because I have already met with Mary without Sarah at the beginning of the session, Mary does not have to interrupt Sarah to "correct" Sarah's version of the events; Mary has already given her version to me and has felt that I understood and accepted her view and concerns.

T: What was she mad at you about?
S: I didn't finish my dinner, and she hates it when I waste food.
T: Oh, so that made you mad, and then you hit her? (I offer my understanding or hypothesis of what happened, a possible "why.")
S: No, I wasn't mad; I was worried what she'd do to punish me.
T: Then what happened? (I accept her statement and move to deepen and explore her experience.)
S: After we cleaned up dinner, she told me to come into the living room to help her clean up.
T: Oh, so that's when you got mad at her?

Note: The therapist does not have to be right. Expressing a tentative opinion and trying to understand Sarah shows that I am interested in Sarah, that I value her and her experience. Past experiences have taught the child to believe that the child is not loved, loveable, valued, or valuable. As described below, it is experiences that are therapeutic and it is the parents' loving attitude and connection with their child that helps create new healing experiences. Being loving is related to commitment. It reflects the degree of commitment that the parent has for the child.

ACCEPTING the other person's view, feelings, and understanding leads to learning what is driving the behavior. Discovering the meaning of an event, situation, or interchange for the person is a major element of treatment. If the therapist only tries to address or change the surface behavior it may end up in a battle or argument because the underlying concern or emotion that is the motivating factor is not addressed. By accepting what the person says, by going deeper and addressing what is driving the behavior, you will be more effective in the end. Addressing only the surface behavior is a lot like playing that arcade game, "Wack-A-Mole," in which more moles keep popping up; the only way to make the moles stop is to shut down the underlying mechanism.

CURIOSITY refers to asking questions in order to develop EMPATHY. It is a nonjudgmental unconditional interest about the inner life of the other. It is an unconditional interest in the other's intentions, thoughts, feelings, desires, and dreams. The idea is to ask questions so that there is an understanding about what is really going on below the surface. For example, while the child may look angry, often what is driving the behavior is fear. While lying may look sneaky and deceitful, it is often driven by overwhelming shame. Shame causes one to want to hide. Lying is just another way of hiding. The point is that when one understands with both cognitive and affective dimensions (has empathy) and identifies what is causing the person's behavior, one's feelings about the person will reflect this understanding. Then, actions are much more likely to be therapeutic because the motivating feelings the person may need help managing are being addressed. The meaning ascribed to behavior influences reactions; "liar" evokes different feelings than a person who feels "bad, defective, unlovable," and full of shame. An "angry and violent" child creates different and negative feelings than a "terrified" child. In the same vein, the therapist feels differently toward a parent who seems overly harsh and punitive than one whose intention is to help the child learn to act in a way that will help the child be successful in school because the parent "knows" the child can do it.

INTERSUBJECTIVITY

As previously described, intersubjectivity is shared affect, intention, and attention. Intersubjectivity can be concordant, when all three elements are in accord, or it can be discordant. In addition, intersubjective experiences can be positive or negative. It is concordant intersubjective experiences that are therapeutic. It forms the central process by which therapeutic interventions are effective or not. The therapist's awareness of the status of the intersubjective experience is essential for ensuring that interactions are therapeutic. When an interchange seems to be going awry, it is useful to consider which element of the intersubjective experience is discordant. Very often it will be that the intentions are discordant. An example may serve to illustrate this. In this example, the therapist is talking with a single parent, Dave, about his son, Brian, age twelve. Dave appears to be rather critical and punitive, and the therapist wants to help Dave focus on what is driving Brian's behavior rather than on surface behavior. However, in this example, the interchange does not go well.

> Dave: I just got Brian's five-week report and it is awful. He's failing math and ELA and is barely passing his other subjects. I told him if he doesn't do better, he'd be grounded until he does. I am so mad at him.
> Therapist: OK, so you want him to get better grades. Why did he do so poorly? (Problem solving rather than looking deeper)
> D: Because he doesn't study and missed a lot of homework.
> T: I see; so you figure you can get him to study more and do his homework if he's grounded and has no TV or computer or games?
> D: Exactly!
> T: You've done this before, and it hasn't worked. Why do you think it will this time? (Problem solving. The therapist is now beginning to feel annoyed with Dave not getting what they've talked about before)
> D: What else should I do? (Dave starts to become defensive; no surprise)
> T: I think you have to understand that the way to get him to do well is by having a better relationship with him. "It's about connections not compliance," is what I say. (This problem solving intellectualized statement has a strong undertone of blame. Perhaps the therapist is feeling that he has to defend Brian. This is where the therapist could have moved the interchange into a concordant intersubjective experience.)
> D: What, so I'm supposed to be his buddy and ignore his bad grades? (And now, Dave and the therapist are on opposite sides of the fence and are arguing. They are not engaged with each other in a concordant manner.)
> T: No. What I mean is the way to get good grades is to focus on having a relationship with him so that he wants to do well. Right now he feels you are forcing him to do well. (Here the therapist is beginning to act as Brian's advocate, defending him against his father.)
> D: So what's wrong with that?
> T: What's wrong with that is that now you are both in a control battle with Brian's grades. Privileges being the ammunition, you each are shooting at each other. (And the therapist is in a control battle of sorts with the father.)

It goes downhill from here. While what the therapist is saying may be on target, the interchange is not concordant on the dimensions of intention or emotion. The therapist appears to be set on "explaining" what Dave should do, and Dave appears to be set on defending his approach. They don't have joint shared intention. It is also likely that Dave may be feeling blamed by the therapist and that the therapist may be feeling annoyed that Dave just doesn't "get it." Maybe the therapist is thinking, "Brian is a good kid, if only Dave would see that." So the therapist begins to try to act as Brian's advocate and defender. This may then lead to an interpersonal conflict between the therapist and Dave when the conflict between caring about Brian and wanting to have him get good grades should be intrapersonal (within Dave).

So, what would have been a better approach? The following example illustrates how focusing on the elements of intersubjectivity and what is discordant can lead to a more effective interchange.

> Dave: I just got Brian's five-week report and it is awful. He's failing math and ELA and is barely passing his other subjects. I told him if he doesn't do better he'd be grounded until he does. I am so mad at him.
> Therapist: You sound upset. (The therapist moves to affect)
> D: You bet I am. I know he can do better; he's just lazy!

(Now, the therapist could argue with Dave about whether or not Brian is lazy or if he just feels so bad about himself that he acts in a way to confirm his self image, or maybe that Brian's past experiences have led him to feel nothing he does matters, so why try? However, instead the therapist will stay focused on Dave for now to deepen their concordant intersubjectivity and keep all three dimensions in sync.)

> T: You sound disappointed or hurt, maybe that Brian isn't doing better.
> D: I am disappointed. I know he can do better; he's a smart kid. He could have a great future if he applied himself. (Dave is now talking more softly, and he appears more somber.)
> T: You really love Brian and want him to do well, don't you?
> D: Yes, I'm his Dad. I've been trying for four years now, and I just get so frustrated sometimes that nothing I do makes a difference. What am I going to do?
> T: Let's figure it together, OK? I'm sure we can come up with something.
> D: OK
> T: You said Brian is a bright kid and could do so much better. What is your guess on why he doesn't? (The therapist has now created joint intention and attention: "we will figure this out together.")
> D: I just think he's lazy.
> T: Education is really important to you, and you've said that he could go far with his brains, so what would make such a kid be lazy? (Here the therapist accepts Dave's view and tries to go deeper by asking a question, by being curious.)
> D: Maybe he never had anyone teach him how to work?
> T: You mean that maybe, because he was so neglected as a young child, he never learned to put forth effort and all those foster homes he was in never made him feel anything mattered or that he mattered?
> D: I never thought about it that way, but yeah, that makes sense, the poor kid. So what do I do now?

T: Well, let's figure out how to help him feel he's capable and see what you see in him.
D: Well, punishing him like I've been doing doesn't work. All it probably did, I now see, is confirm that he's a failure and that I'm mad at him. How do I make that up to him? (Because of the safety created by the therapist, Dave is able to explore what he's been doing and consider alternatives.)

Within this concordant intersubjective experience, Dave and the therapist have achieved two things. First, they have deepened their relationship. The therapist understands Dave better, and Dave feels the therapist wants to help him by understanding him. The therapist has modeled with Dave what the therapist may want Dave to do with Brian. Second, they co-created a new meaning for Brian's poor grades that leads to a different and more effective set of behaviors.

REFLECTIVE CAPACITY

Reflective capacity refers to the capacity to simultaneously be in an experience and to be able to think about that experience. Peter Fonagy (Fonagy et al. 2002) describes this as mentalizing. It means having a mental representation of self, other, and the relationship. This mental representation allows one to anticipate the other's potential actions, feelings, and thoughts and then act accordingly. It is the basis for empathy, the capacity to see and feel with the other. Obviously the therapist must have a well-developed reflective function. One of the goals of treatment is to enhance and develop the caregiver's reflective capacity and to develop and enhance the child's reflective capacity. The reflective function is necessary for impulse control. It provides that half second of pause, so one can consider a response within the context of what one believes the other's intention, feelings, and thoughts are. A brief example will serve to illustrate the reflective function. In this example that occurred near the end of treatment, Aaron, age fourteen, is describing to me how his birth mother hurt him and his siblings.

Aaron: And then Emma (his birth mom) would hit Lindsey and Bobby. She'd use the metal fry pan and it was horrible. Oh, Dr. Art, I'm not changing the subject, I just want you to know how my mom hurt me and my sister and brothers. OK?

In this example, Aaron describes what happened and it also exemplifies the operation of the reflective function. In order for Aaron to make the last statement, "Oh, Dr. Art, I'm not changing the subject . . ." he had to have a mental representation of me, the discussion, and his intentions. While talking, he realized that I might assume he was changing the subject by talking about his siblings and not himself. So, he tells me what his intention is and assures me he is not changing the subject. To do this Aaron had to have a mental representation of how I think and of our relationship.

AFFECTIVE/REFLECTIVE DIALOGUE

An affective/reflective dialogue can be described as a conversation that contains emotional, reflective, and cognitive elements. It is a relaxed and meandering dialogue that has a story-telling quality to it. An affective/reflective dialogue is not a rational discussion or a lecture. The client actively participates in the dialogue, and the back-and-forth or give-and-take quality of this dialogue is quite evident. There is emotional engagement in this dialogue. All events from the person's life that seem related to the discussion are explored openly. Serious events, traumatic events, or behavior do not elicit a serious or lecture tone because that could cause the person to disengage from the dialogue. This relaxed and meandering dialogue often side-steps resistance since the client is an active participant in the dialogue and the resulting co-creation of meaning.

It is the therapist's responsibility to set the rhythm and tone for the session, to set the PACE of treatment. When defensiveness or "resistance" is evident, it is the therapist's responsibility to respond to it in a sensitive manner. The therapist may want take responsibility for causing the "resistance" or "defensiveness," in that it is possible that had the therapist been more attuned to the client's subtle emotional cues, the therapist may have responded sooner and in a way to avoid the resistance or defensiveness. Defensiveness may be caused by the client not experiencing a sense of safety and security in the therapy setting, but rather fear, and the client may experience the lack of a secure base from which exploration can occur. Often this may occur earlier in treatment rather than in later phases when the therapist has a more attuned sense of the client and the client experiences the therapist's intentions as being to help the client. When defensiveness or "resistance" is evident, the therapist relies on PACE. The therapist accepts the client's resistance, is curious about it, has empathy for the resistance, and weaves it into the affective/reflective dialogue. Since the therapist has no "agenda" or hidden motive for the discussion, no lecture to give or point to make, there is no "pressure" to explore any trauma or event as these are simply a few aspects of the person's story, all of which are interesting to the therapist. Eventually the client will feel comfortable exploring any aspect because the therapist has created the necessary safety and security, the secure base required for exploration. The creation of the secure base requires an affective/reflective dialogue so that intentions and emotions are evident and explored; both the client's and the therapist's intentions are part of the dialogue. Another element of this dialogue is that it demonstrates to the client that the therapist is interested in and values the client.

The affective/reflective dialogue may occur within one dialogue, or it may occur across a session or sessions. For example, sessions often begin with a focus on the experience of specific situations that occurred in the past or that are occurring in the moment. These experiences are explored, and the dialogue about the experience between the parent and child or parent and therapist deepens as the emotional content is integrated with the cognitive content. As the session draws to an end, the therapist leads the dialogue into a more reflective dialogue about the experiences explored and about the session itself. The focus of this reflection is to highlight the child's and parent's strengths, including the child's developing ability to turn to the caregiver for help. In individual sessions with just the parent, the focus of this reflection will be on connecting past family of origin dynamics to the present and on the parent's successes and accomplishments as a parent. In this manner affect regulation and reflective functioning are developed and advanced in each session.

COMMITMENT

The therapist's commitment is to the family, to help the family become a "happier" place. To achieve this, the therapist may find that the therapist's primary commitment will have to be to the parents since they are the keystone for healing and a successful outcome. Many therapists trained as child therapists find themselves in the awkward position of feeling, "If only the parents would get a grip, this child would be fine." What then often happens is that the therapist begins to feel and act as the child's advocate, speaking for the child and trying to convince the parents to be better parents. This path frequently leads to an impasse or to the family discontinuing treatment. As described above in the discussion about "resistance," if the parents have difficulties that impair their ability to create a healing place, the therapist will have to use PACE and the affective/reflective dialogue to create a secure base that will allow the parents to explore what is interfering with their being the way they would like to be. The therapist will have to use PACE to join with, accept, understand, and support the parents so that the parents can accept, understand, and support their child. Whatever the therapist wishes the parents to be able to do with their child the therapist has to be able to do with the parents.

Commitment can be described as the extent to which the caregiver is motivated to have an enduring relationship with a specific child. The highly committed caregiver shows evidence of caring for this child. The therapist will have to evaluate and, when necessary, explore the caregiver's commitment to the child. If necessary, the therapist may have to work with the caregivers to determine if the level of commitment can be strengthened and enhanced. Research shows that the best predictor of placement stability is the caregiver's commitment (Dozier & Lindheim 2006). Experiences in treatment cannot deepen unless there is a sense of safety and security. Caregivers create this for the child primarily through their commitment to the child, which is communicated largely in a non-verbal manner. Commitment is an emotional connection. It is an experience of deep emotional connection to the child and that one's life as a parent would be substantially diminished if the child were not part of the parent's life.

Some questions that can be used to gauge a caregiver's commitment to a particular child are (from Dozier & Lindheim, 2006):

- How much would you miss (child's name) if (child's name) had to leave?
- How do you think your relationship with (child's name) is affecting (child's name) right now?
- How do you think your relationship with (child's name) will affect (child's name) in the long-term?
- What do you want for (child's name) right now?
- What do you want for (child's name) in the future?

Before beginning treatment and at the beginning of each session, the therapist assesses the primary caregiver's readiness to be an attachment figure for the child. While not exclusively relating to commitment, this is a significant element of commitment. The therapist's assessment will involve the caregiver's overall readiness and ability to provide safety, which is influenced by the caregiver's pattern of attachment, relationship history, commitment, insightfulness, reflective capabilities, and other factors. In addition, the assessment includes an evaluation of the caregiver's immediate ability to provide PACE when the child is engaged in treatment. The child is never put in a position of lowering the child's defenses if the therapist is not confident that the caregiver can respond in a supportive and therapeutic manner. This is one component of providing emotional safety in sessions. In those instances in which there is some doubt regarding the caregiver's ability to not be shaming, blaming, or overly critical or doubt regarding the caregiver's ability or willingness to enhance the creation of a secure base, the therapist will work primarily with the caregiver. In this work with the caregiver, the therapist will be focused on helping the parent feel safe enough to engage in the necessary exploration to resolve what may be impediments to the caregiver's ability at this time.

An example may be helpful at this point. In this example, the parent is talking with the therapist without the child. The parent, Delores, came in quite angry at her daughter and in no mood to be understanding or accepting of the child.

Therapist: You seem upset, Delores. What's the matter?
Delores: I've told that girl a thousand times, when you yawn, cover your mouth, when you sneeze, cover your nose, when you're eating, don't talk with your mouth full. These are disgusting habits. Emily does these things on purpose just to tick me off; she knows how I feel.

Note: Delores is not in any state to work with Emily or to try to go beyond Emily's behavior, so the therapist will talk with Delores about this as long as it takes until Delores is able to use PLACE and focus in an accepting, supportive, and understanding manner on what may be driving Emily's behavior. That may mean that all of today's session is exclusively the therapist and Delores, and maybe even several sessions afterwards. The therapist has to be an "ACE" therapist for Delores, accepting her, being curious, and having empathy for her. This will create and maintain the alliance necessary to create the safety, and the secure base, necessary for exploration, integration, and healing.

T: So you are upset, angry maybe, because she's just trying to make you mad?
D: That's right; she can be a real brat sometimes.
T: We've talked about this before and how much these things bother you. I wonder why she'd *try* to make you mad.
D: She's just a brat; she likes seeing me lose my tempter.
T: How do you feel when you lose your temper?
D: Oh, well, me?
T: Yes, how do you feel when you lose your temper and yell at her?
D: Awful and stupid. How can I let this five year old get under my skin so badly?
T: You sound unhappy with what goes on at home?
D: Well, I am. This is not how I expect to be as Emily's mother. I just don't know why I get so angry at her.
T: You know, I was thinking the same thing. I was remembering something you described a few weeks ago. Can I tell you?

The therapist will now try to go deeper with Delores and asks permission. The therapist is using the "lead" part of the follow-lead-follow component.

D: Sure, what was it?

T: I remember you describing how Timmy has these tantrums and how he'll even break stuff, but you don't seem to get so upset with that? You seem more upset with Emily's behavior than Timmy's.
D: (small laugh and smile). That's true, I really don't get upset at Timmy, and when you put it that way, it does seem kinda strange that Emily's little behaviors would get to me so much.
T: Yes, I wonder why that would be. What was it like in your home when you were growing up about things like Emily did?
D: Oh, we lived on a small farm in rural South Carolina and Momma and Poppa always made us mind our manners. The worst thing you could do, even worse than getting bad grades or messing up a chore, was being rude to them; that'd get you a real heavy punishment; you'd not be able to sit down for a week if you did that!
T: I get it. So manners are really important for your family. And you learned about that from the time you were born I bet.
D: That's right, from day one.
T: But Emily's only been in your home about a year, is that right?
D: That's right. Maybe I am too hard on her. I mean I don't want to be as harsh as my momma was with me and the others. Emily's already had a hard life. I love my momma, but I don't always want to be like she did.

Note: So now Delores has a deeper understanding of her own feelings and how her history and family experiences affect her being a mother. With this insight she will be better able to choose a course of action in relation to Emily that is therapeutic and that considers Emily's history of trauma.

INSIGHTFULNESS

Insightfulness is related to the reflective function described above. To be insightful means to look within, "in" "sight." Insight involves the ability to look within and to more deeply understand one's self, one's motives and intentions, and how these have been shaped by past and current experiences, relationships, and events. Insight allows the therapist to better understand what emotions are being activated by the therapist's past experiences and which emotions are being activated by the current experiences.

Developing insightfulness among family members is one of the important tasks of the therapist practicing Dyadic Developmental Psychotherapy. The therapist accomplishes this through the use of the affective/reflective dialogue, by the co-creation of meanings, by follow-lead-follow, by interactive repair, and by the verbal/non-verbal dialogue. The affective/reflective dialogue along with the verbal/non-verbal dialogue is one method by which insight is achieved. This dialogue with its emotional and reflective components is how the client achieves greater self-knowledge. When entered into, this dialogue is how new and more helpful meanings of experiences are co-created. This dialogue is led by the therapist in the follow-lead-follow format. Interactive repair ensures that the inevitable mistakes that occur in this process are owned and accepted and then explored and repaired. Interactive repair has the effect of reducing shame. It is within the safety of the secure base that the exploration necessary to achieve integration and healing can occur. This integration and healing occurs by exploring current experiences and their connections to past experiences. By exploring how the past is alive in the present, the therapist assists the client in achieving deeper insightfulness.

COHERENT NARRATIVE & THE CO-CREATION OF MEANING

The creation of a coherent autobiographical narrative is one marker of mental health. A personal narrative changes over time, but it is this narrative that gives meaning to one's life and experiences. Those with a secure pattern of attachment are able to tell a coherent story about their life, regardless of how difficult that life may have been. A coherent autobiographical narrative reflects the integration of the left brain hemisphere function of containing explicit memories with right hemisphere where affect and implicit memories are located. Trauma interferes with this integration. Without this integration, one's sense of self with a past, present, and future can become distorted, vague, and disconnected. Children who have experienced complex trauma frequently have disjointed, split-off, and dissociated autobiographical narratives. The episodic and emotional elements of the trauma are split off and disconnected from each other. While the emotional sequelae of the trauma are clearly evident in the child's behavior, the child is not aware of this. Revisiting the trauma in detail and in a titrated manner so that the emotions are experienced in the safe and secure setting of the therapy session and in the home allows for the integration of emotional and episodic memories and the conscious awareness of how these events and feelings are operating in the present. As described previously, this is insightfulness. It is this insightfulness that provides an important healing dimension to treatment. Once dissociated elements are integrated into a coherent autobiographical narrative, the child is able to manage the underlying emotions and engage the reflective function to select an appropriate and self-advancing response.

The therapist practicing Dyadic Developmental Psychotherapy focuses on helping the child develop this coherence and on guiding the parents to help create this coherence. There are many activities that can assist the child in exploring and telling the child's story to achieve greater integration and coherence. These activities include drawing, playing with puppets or stuffed animals, reading children's books, and psychodrama. The use of actual court documents, adoption summaries, and child protection investigation reports can also be quite useful. These materials are used in a "titrated" manner to evoke some emotion to help achieve integration, but not so much emotion as to overwhelm the child or the parent. As in all aspects of treatment, the therapist is attuned to the child's response to these materials and activities, and they are only used and continued when the child shows that the child feels safe within the experience.

It is important to remember that experiences, in and of themselves, have no meaning until those experiences are made meaningful through narrative. The meanings ascribed to early experiences affect the inner working model and sense of self as competent and worthy or as defective and unlovable. It is through telling stories, the creation of a narrative, together with a significant other that shared meaning is co-created. It is shared meanings, shared experiences, and shared emotions that create a shared relationship.

CO-REGULATION OF EMOTIONS

Children and adults with difficult histories often have not received the necessary experiences that would allow them to effectively regulate their own emotions. In most typical circumstances, a parent first regulates the infant's emotional world and so regulates the infant's emotional experiences. The "good enough" parent provides stimulation to activate the infant but is careful not to over-stimulate. The "good enough" parent sooths the upset infant and reduces distress. In this fashion, the parent regulates the infant and young child's level of arousal and emotional experiences. Over time the child begins to internalize this shared co-regulation of affect and becomes self-regulating. The sequence: first the parent regulates the child, then the child is able to achieve emotional regulation with the parent's help, and then the child can self-regulate.

Children and adults who have difficulty regulating their emotions need help to do so, and the therapist begins by doing this with the client. By co-regulating the client's level of arousal and affect, the client will become able to do so independently. The therapist does this by keeping the level of affect within what Briere & Scott (2006) call the "therapeutic window." There must be some emotion present in the dialogue to make the dialogue meaningful and therapeutic, to help achieve integration, but not so much that the client becomes dysregulated.

Touch may be used to help in the co-regulation of affect, if provided by a caregiver in a supportive, caring, nurturing manner. The parent may be encouraged to touch the child during the session when it is called for by what is happening in the session and if the child is receptive to being touched. Touch may occur in many different ways and should be based on what will be comforting for the child. For example, squeezing the child's hand or putting an arm around the child if the child is sad or anxious, playfully touching the child during laughter or joking, and giving the child a hug when the child is in distress while recounting an unpleasant or difficult experience or to express support and pride in what the child has accomplished. The therapist may also use touch with a client to express concern, support, or to share an emotion. For example, the therapist may rest a hand on the client's arm or shoulder to express support. If the child is not comfortable with some particular touch, it is stopped immediately and responded to with PACE and interactive repair.

FOLLOW-LEAD-FOLLOW

Follow-Lead-Follow describes the ebb and flow of the dialogue within the Dyadic Developmental Psychotherapy session. This framework is designed to encourage client engagement and to increase the client's sense of safety, security, and personal control. The therapist begins by using the PACE framework, accepting what the client says. The therapist follows the client's flow of dialogue and emotion and stays in step with the client. The objective here is to, metaphorically, walk with and next to the client. This helps create a secure base by providing the client with acceptance and a concordant intersubjective experience. Client and therapist are sharing affect and are attending to the same thing. Intentions are conjoint and complementary, so the therapist is interested in what the client is interested in at the moment. The client will feel valued because the therapist is focusing on what the client finds of interest. Once the dialogue has moved along to some degree, the therapist can then begin to lead the client into a related path that has a different trajectory. For example, the therapist may begin to note how this situation is similar to one that occurred in the past or comment on what the client may have been feeling. The therapist leads the discussion deeper. Once on this new trajectory, the therapist again follows the client and the cycle continues.

Another example of the follow-lead-follow approach is that children with traumatic histories often have limited abilities to connect the trauma to words. The therapist first engages with the client around what is on the client's mind. The therapist often takes the lead early in treatment to cautiously provide the words for the child, and then, if the words are acknowledged by the child as accurate representations of the child's experience and inner life, the therapist may "speak for" the child to the caregiver. The therapist may put into words what the therapist believes is the child's experience. The following example illustrates these processes.

Parent: He had such a fit yesterday when I brought him to a new sitter for the day while I went to work
Therapist: Billy was really upset.
P: I don't know why? He wouldn't tell me.
T: Billy, do you know what upset you yesterday?
Billy: (as he buries his head under the couch pillow he mumbles in a pitiful voice) Sorry.
T: You sound upset Billy; can you say what upset you so?
B: (he remains quite and under the cushion).
T: Say, Billy, would it be OK if I pretended to be you and talk for you to your mom?
B: (from under the cushion) Yes.
T: If I get something wrong, will you let me know?
B: OK
T: OK, I'm gonna talk for Billy now. "Mom, I got so scared when you brought me to that place yesterday. I thought you were going to leave me there and never come back."

The therapist's non-verbal expressions, tone of voice, and cadence are congruent with the words, and this will often allow the child to experience the dialogue with the parent as if the child had actually said the words to the parent.

INTERACTIVE REPAIR

Interactive repair (Tronick 1989, Tronick 2005) describes how the therapist or parent responds to the inevitable breaches that occur in any relationship during the ebb and flow of experience. Interactive repair refers to the adults' actions to repair the relationship and to emotionally reconnect with and reestablish an attuned relationship with the child after there has been a breach in the relationship. Interactive repair is the process by which a caregiver repairs some misattunement in the relationship in a manner that reduces shame. Interactive repair leads to the development of greater capacity to experience negative emotions without resultant shame and dysregulation. Interactive repair requires a caregiver who is sensitive and collaborative. When the caregiver helps the child recover from a negative affective state, the amount of shame experienced is reduced. When the caregiver engages in interactive repair on a fairly consistent basis, the child develops an internal experience of self as effective, that the child's intentions are positive, and that distress is reparable.

The healing dimension of interactive repair is that it reduces shame. Interactive repair can help a child progress developmentally from a shame-based identity to the experience of healthy and appropriate guilt. The parent setting a limit may cause the break in the relationship, specifically in some element of shared intersubjectivity, usually a discontinuity in shared emotion or joint complementary intention. A breach in the relationship can also be caused by an adult misunderstanding the child or missing important emotional cues. The disruption in the relationship that occurs may lead to the child experiencing shame. The cycle of experiencing positive affect following negative experiences teaches the child that negative emotions can be tolerated and resolved and that the relationship can be repaired. Over time as the healthy parent reestablishes attunement, the child begins to experience the self as intrinsically good, although as one who occasionally does "bad" things. It is this movement from feeling that one is bad to feeling that one is good but does bad things that is at the core of the developmental step from shame to guilt.

The therapist or parent uses PACE to initiate interactive repair. The core component in this process is an acceptance of the child and recognition by the adult that it is the adult's responsibility to initiate and repair of the relationship. Children who have experienced long histories of neglect or abuse have not experienced interactive repair in any consistent manner. As a result, these children have a pervasive sense of shame, which is about who the child is and leads to wanting to hide. Guilt, which is about what was done, leads to wanting to confess or fix the error. These children require intensive experiences of interactive repair at home and in the therapy setting to begin to remove the crippling elements of overwhelming shame. An example will serve to illustrate this point.

Amos was ten years old. He was adopted when he was six after a three-year stint in six different foster homes, some of which had been nearly as abusive as his birth family. His adoptive father was abusive, and his adoptive mother (Erica) left the father when Amos was nine. Amos now lives with his adoptive mother and brother. In addition to Reactive Attachment Disorder and complex trauma, Amos had been diagnosed by a child psychiatrist with Bipolar I Disorder and was on several different psychotropic medications. Amos would often pull out his hair and pick at sores and his body until he bled. The following interchange took place in a second or third session, before I knew Amos or his mother very well. We are all sitting on a couch with Amos between me and his mother. This example illustrates the therapist initiating interactive repair.

Therapist: That must have been so scary for you when your birth mom and dad used to fight with each other like they did.

Amos: I guess (he is looking straight ahead, without much affect present, except, as I noted later on the tape of the session, his tapping foot).
Therapist: Your mom was telling me that your birth parents used to hit each other, and lots of times one or both got really hurt, and the police showed up.
A: Um.
Erica: Yes, that's what the social workers told me. They said when the police showed up Amos would be hiding under a bed or in a closet.
T: Oh, Amos, do you remember that?
A: Um.
T: You must have been so scared to hear and see that. (I now notice that Amos has picked his nose and is wiping the blood on my left shirt sleeve.)

Note: Since it is the therapist's job to maintain a healing pace, I see what is happening as being caused by my missing cues that Amos was giving me earlier that he did not want to talk about this topic. Since I did not notice those cues or respond, Amos has to raise his voice, so to speak, for me to hear him. Once he was wiping blood on my shirt, I finally "heard" him.

T: (turning toward Amos and catching his eye). Oh, Amos, I am so sorry, I didn't realize how upsetting this must be for you. I should have noticed sooner. Do you want to stop talking about this?
A: Yes!
T: OK, that's fine; do you think you could say that to me? Could you say to me, "Dr. Art, I don't want to talk about my birth mom anymore!"
A: OK, Dr. Art, I don't wanna talk about this anymore.
T: OK, let's talk about something else. What should we talk about?

NON-VERBAL AND VERBAL DIALOGUES

Treatment of the child has a significant non-verbal dimension. Often the trauma took place at a pre-verbal stage and/or may be dissociated from explicit memory because of its overwhelming nature. As a result, childhood maltreatment and resultant trauma create barriers to successful engagement and treatment of these children. Treatment interventions are designed to create experiences of safety and security (the safe base from which exploration can occur) and concordant intersubjectivity so that the child is emotionally engaged and can explore and resolve past trauma. One element of this is affective attunement, which is the same process that involves non-verbal communication between a caregiver and child during attachment facilitating interactions (Siegel, 2001). The therapist and caregivers' attunement results in co-regulation of the child's emotions so that the emotions are now manageable. Cognitive restructuring interventions are designed to help the child develop secondary mental representations of traumatic events, which enable the child to integrate these events and develop a coherent autobiographical narrative. Non-verbal communication, involving eye contact, tone of voice, cadence, volume, touch, gestures, and movement, is another element of treatment and constitutes a part of affective attunement.

A significant proportion of communication, particularly of an affective and emotional nature is non-verbal. Quite often the manner in which something is said can communicate more and be more important than the actual words. A gentle touch, a shared smile or tear, or a look of concern and worry may create a deeper shared experience than words alone. When words and non-verbal communications are discordant, the non-verbal elements rather than the words are believed. For these reasons, the Dyadic Developmental Psychotherapy therapist pays particular attention to the non-verbal cues occurring in the family during treatment and will often comment on these non-verbal statements to deepen the experience and to further develop insightfulness and reflective functions.

In this example the therapist is talking with the parents and child.

Brenda: (speaking to her son Armond) I remember when we went to Russia to get you. You were four years old.
Armond: Tell the story, tell the story!!
Brenda: (opening up the photo album) Here we are at the orphanage in the garden with you.
Armond: (pointing to a woman in the picture) Who is that?
Ralph: That's Irina, one of the orphanage ladies.
Armond: OH!
Brenda: That was such a happy day (begins to tear up).
Therapist: I wonder what your tears are about Brenda.
Brenda: (in a halting voice as tears begin to fall) I just see that picture and then I think about my little boy in that orphanage all by himself with no one there to hug him. He was all alone.
Therapist: You wish you could have been there for Armond.
Brenda: (crying hard now) Yes, I wish I'd been there when he was born and that he'd never had to be there (hugs Armond, who is hugging her and also crying).

SUMMARY

Dyadic Developmental Psychotherapy has as its core, or central therapeutic mechanism for treatment success, the maintenance of a contingent, collaborative, sensitive, reflective, and affectively attuned relationship between therapist and child, between caregiver and child, and between therapist and caregiver. The creation and maintenance of concordant intersubjectivity is central to the process, which occurs through the application of PACE. Dyadic Developmental Psychotherapy focuses on and relies upon the intersubjective sharing and joint development and organization of emotional experience. What distinguishes Dyadic Developmental Psychotherapy from other methods of family treatment with children is the strong emphasis on maintaining an intersubjective relationship with the parent and child, deep acceptance of each family member's affect and experience, non-judgmental curiosity about the meaning the family member may have given to events and situations, and greater emphasis on experience and process rather than on verbalization and content. The practice of Dyadic Developmental Psychotherapy requires the therapist to become affectively attuned with the parent and the child to maintain joint attention and shared complementary intentions. Dyadic Developmental Psychotherapy requires a greater use of self in both the here-and-now experience of the family member as well as in the expression of that experience to the family member, than do some other forms of treatment such as Cognitive Behavioral Therapy, Trauma-focused CBT, Behavior Modification approaches, or several other forms of family therapy.

Dyadic Developmental Psychotherapy seeks to remediate the negative working models of clients that are interfering with their functioning, using experiential methods that have several important and overlapping dimensions:

- modeling the healthy attachment cycle,
- reducing shame,
- safe and nurturing physical contact that is containing,
- re-experiencing or re-visiting the affect associated with the trauma in order to integrate the experience and not dissociate, and
- the interpersonal regulation of affect.

Dyadic Developmental Psychotherapy interventions flow from several theoretical and empirical lines. Attachment theory (Bowlby, 1980, 1988) provides the theoretical foundation for Dyadic Developmental Psychotherapy. Early trauma disrupts the normally developing attachment system by creating distorted internal working models of self, others, and caregivers. This is one rationale for treatment in addition to the necessity for sensitive caregiving. As O'Connor & Zeanah (2003, 235) have stated, "A more puzzling case is that of an adoptive/foster caregiver who is 'adequately' sensitive but the child exhibits attachment disorder behavior; it would seem unlikely that improving parental sensitive responsiveness (in already sensitive parent) would yield positive changes in the parent-child relationship.'' Treatment is necessary to directly address the rigid and dysfunctional internalized working models that traumatized children with attachment disorders have developed.

In this chapter we have outlined fourteen major components of Dyadic Developmental Psychotherapy. By now the reader should have a good understanding of each of these elements and how each is important in treatment. Succeeding chapters will discuss how these components are differentially used, depending on the phase of treatment and on other factors.

Chapter 5

Phases

This chapter describes the phases of treatment. These are not rigidly defined phases; rather these phases provide a framework for understanding the relationship, experience, and the application of the various components of Dyadic Developmental Psychotherapy that occur in a cyclical manner. The reader may think of these as processes that occur in a repetitive, overlapping, and sequential manner. For example, healing occurs throughout treatment, not just at one point at the end of treatment. Each phase requires the presence of the preceding phase; healing requires integration, which is built on exploration, which requires a secure base, which is built on the foundation of an alliance. These phases may be thought of a similar to the phases of the moon, which occur in a cyclical manner. A colleague described it this way: Dyadic Developmental Psychotherapy is "a coherent whole, with all parts equally important and always there. Sometimes though one part is seen (or focused on, or is visible to others) and is lit up, or in the foreground. That stays around a while before another part becomes visible. What you see depends on the relationship" (Hudson, J., 2010). The phases occur in a repetitive manner, much like a spiral. Exploration and integration can lead to a more secure alliance, which will allow for deeper exploration and further integration and healing. Healing often allows for a stronger alliance to develop, which will facilitate further integration.

An understanding of the different phases of treatment will guide the Dyadic Developmental Psychotherapist in the application of the principles, elements, and components of Dyadic Developmental Psychotherapy described earlier. While the general principles remain constant (the primacy of relationship and experience, repair of relationship, intersubjectivity), each phase requires a different mix of elements with a shifting emphasis on the various components.

MAIN COMPONENTS OF DYADIC DEVELOPMENTAL PSYCHOTHERAPY

- Therapist use of self
- Process focused: It's about connections not compliance
- PLACE and PACE
- Intersubjectivity
- Reflective Capacity
- Affective/Reflective dialogue
- Commitment
- Insightfulness
- Coherent narrative
- Co-regulation of emotions
- Co-creation of meanings
- Follow-lead-follow
- Interactive repair
- Nonverbal-verbal dialogue

It is the application of the various elements of Dyadic Developmental Psychotherapy in a differential manner that is the art of this treatment. It is most useful to think of the phases as occurring in a cyclical iterative manner. One phase may last several sessions, and many phases may be present in one session. Healing may begin in the very first session, for example. In this chapter I provide some guidance in the application of this art. The material presented here is based on the work of Daniel Hughes as interpreted and reorganized into a different framework by me. What I have tried to do is take the materials developed by Hughes (see Hughes, 2007, for example) and place it into a new frame while maintaining fidelity to his work.

After beginning with a brief description of each phase, I will describe some of the markers that indicate the beginning of a new phase. Then I will describe the major challenges and opportunities within each phase. The differential application of the basic components of Dyadic Developmental Psychotherapy will be described. Finally, I will identify certain difficulties that may arise and approaches to addressing those difficulties.

An alliance is necessary to create and maintain a secure base. A secure base is built on a reciprocal, responsive, emotionally attuned relationship, safety. A secure base is necessary to begin exploration as it provides the sense of safety and security necessary to undertake exploration. Exploration is necessary to achieve integration. Integration is the basis for healing.

PHASES

- Developing the alliance
- Maintaining the alliance (developing a secure base)
- Exploration
- Integration
- Healing

The phases of treatment are defined in terms of attachment theory and child development. The boxed text provides the list of these phases.

DEVELOPING THE ALLIANCE

Developing an alliance, or initial engagement, is the first, necessary step in treatment. Without an alliance, nothing else can happen. It is the foundation on which a secure base is built. Many children and parents are ready to begin treatment. They enter treatment with an expectation that it will be helpful and that the therapist is there on their side to help. In other words, many clients who have a secure state of mind with respect to attachment begin their work with the therapist with basic trust in the relationship and, implicitly, with a beginning alliance with the therapist. On the other hand, clients who have had many unsuccessful treatment experiences, or who have a dismissing, preoccupied, or disorganized state of mind with respect to attachment, and who may have unresolved trauma, are much more cautious and may not experience the therapist as being "on their side." Many of the children I see come into treatment with this as a core area of trauma: an impaired capacity to form and maintain emotionally meaningful, authentic, sensitive, and responsive relationships. With these individuals, the therapist must take substantially longer to develop a working alliance, a therapeutic alliance.

Some therapists may not recognize that this first phase of treatment is treatment, that for a child or parent who has been hurt and who has a damaged capacity to form an alliance, forming an alliance is, in itself, therapy and therapeutic. This phase is the foundation on which treatment success builds, and so it is vital that the therapist not skip over this work to "get to the real or good stuff." This is the good stuff! Building an alliance with a wounded parent or child is therapeutic when such an alliance is built on trust, caring for the other, interest in and concern about the other, a genuine desire to get to know the other, and enjoyment in that experience. Creating concordant intersubjective experiences is the therapy.

While all of the components of Dyadic Developmental Psychotherapy will be used, four have particular salience at this phase of treatment. These four are: intersubjectivity, follow-lead-follow, PACE, and the co-regulation of affect. In this initial phase of treatment the therapist will pay particular attention to co-regulating the emotional state of each member of the family and of the family as a whole. The therapist will use PACE to create concordant intersubjective experiences, which are a primary means of co-regulating affect and of building an alliance.

Primary Tasks

This initial phase has several primary tasks. The goal is to create a secure base for exploration, integration, and healing. Primary tasks in this first phase are:

- Forming a therapeutic alliance
- Developing a "treatment contract." Why are we here? Why are we meeting? What are we doing here?
- Forming initial theories of behavior: the meanings to be explored.
- Creating a secure base.

Forming the Therapeutic Alliance

I sometimes think of children and parents who have been wounded by relationships as being "relationship phobic." They fear intimacy because their past experiences have demonstrated the dangers of relying on others and the dangers of becoming close with another. So, like most people, they act in ways to achieve a level of intimacy that feels familiar or comfortable. If the therapist tries to get "too close," they will find ways to push back. The therapist's challenge is to maintain an emotionally meaningful relationship without causing dysregulation.

How the therapist builds this alliance will largely depend on the therapist's self-awareness and on the therapist's use of self. Building an alliance requires the therapist to be emotionally involved in the ongoing interaction occurring as the relationship develops. Initially it will be the therapist who puts emotional energy into building this alliance and into creating and maintaining concordant intersubjective experiences. A Dyadic Developmental Psychotherapy psychotherapist will use the therapist's self, interests, and the therapist's self-history in a self-aware manner, to create the alliance. One of my colleagues is an art therapist by training. She tends to use a lot of media to engage children. She enjoys art and working with various media such as clay, oil-pastels, water colors, and crayons. Her enjoyment and engagement serves to provide the emotional energy to engage the child in a shared enjoyable experience, which becomes the basis for building the alliance and creating the secure base. I enjoy science, magic, puzzles, and the ocean, so I use these to help create experiences that are engaging. I have many science objects around my office (a radiometer and fossils for example), various puzzles, and lots of sea shells and pictures of sea life from scuba diving trips. Many children enjoy magic and are fascinated by card tricks and disappearing/reappearing objects. This is where self-reflection and sensitivity are important. For example, while many children really enjoy the magic of seeing an object disappear, for other children magic is experienced as their being tricked, and they will become angry. How the therapist uses self has to be done in a sensitive and responsive manner. If a child shows interest in my seashells or a picture I've taken of a sea turtle or dolphin, using follow-lead-follow, we can create a concordant intersubjective experience that is joyful and helps create a stronger alliance. In this example I am describing the use of self in terms of sharing an interest of mine with the child. The actual process involved, not content, is an expression of the therapist's subjective experience of the child and parent. Use of self in the application of Dyadic Developmental Psychotherapy refers to the emotionally meaningful engagement of the therapist with the client; the creation and maintenance of intersubjectivity. In the following example, I am meeting with a child and his father during one of the early sessions. In this example I am focusing on building an alliance with both father and daughter; both have a rather extensive trauma history.

> Barry (Dad): It's been a terrible week. Megan had a lot of tantrums.

Note: While Dad is saying this, Megan, age 11, is sitting there with a scowl on her face and arms crossed.

> Therapist: (to Dad and Megan) Oh, you both had a tough week, it sounds like. Not fun at all.
> Megan: No, I had to stay in my room.
> B: Well, you . . .
> T: (therapist interrupts here) I wonder, Barry, what you two would have done for fun if you'd had a better week?

Note: The therapist intervenes to change the tone of the interaction and move away from a blaming/shaming interaction that both Dad and Megan are used to, and into an interaction that has a more positive emotional tone in order to build a positive experience in the room with them and build the alliance. Now, it is important to emphasize that what I am not saying is that in the early sessions the therapist attempts to avoid conflicts and disagreements.

The therapist does want to interrupt blaming/shaming interactions and try to approach the conflict in a more positive manner. Alternatively, the therapist might note the conflict and then come back to it later in the session. In any event, it is important to not avoid conflicts and differences. It is the manner in which these differences and disagreements are attended to that is important.

B: Hey, if we could have gone to the beach, that would have been fun, right Megan?
M: (still looking sullen, she points to a picture and she mumbles) Is that a shark?
T: Yes, it is. (Follow part of follow-lead-follow)
M: (showing more interest and looking at me for the first time) Weren't you scared?
T: No, the dive leaders made sure we stayed safe and instructed us about what to do and not do while we were down there. (Turning to Barry) What do you think of that picture? (Moving into the lead part of follow-lead-follow)
B: I'd love to take Megan snorkeling; I bet she'd like it.
T: Why don't you ask her?
B: (to Megan) Would you like to go snorkeling?
M: Not if there are sharks around. (Still used to a negative interaction with her dad, she acts in a way, not consciously, of course, to evoke a pattern that feels familiar)
T: Dad, what made you think Megan would like snorkeling? (Here I attempt to keep the focus on something more positive and begin a father-daughter dialogue)
B: Oh, I know she loves the water. She's been on a swim team at the Y for two years now and does great. I'm really proud of how hard she works at it.
M: (now looks at Dad for the first time) Maybe I'd like snorkeling. Would you go with me?

We see here how the therapist uses a personal interest to engage both father and daughter. The therapist uses follow-lead-follow to deepen the experience and move it into a relationship focused interaction and a dialogue between father and daughter.

Developing a Treatment Contract

An essential part of building an alliance is having some common and shared set of expectations regarding, "What are we doing here?" In this phase the therapist wants to begin to develop what may be called a "treatment contract," the shared set of assumptions regarding what it is that will be happening, why, and who is responsible for what. This "contract" can be as elaborate or as informal as is best suited for the family and the work setting. Developing this contract with the parents and caregivers may seem easier because they have initiated the contact, but that isn't necessarily the case. While it is usually true that the parents decide who will be the treatment provider and "contract" with the provider for services, what that actually means may become the source of discord and conflict later in treatment. Developing the treatment contract with the parents begins during the assessment. The manner in which the therapist involves parents begins to set the tone and expectations for future meetings. For example, I usually begin by first meeting with the parents without the child during the assessment. This approach is congruent with Dyadic Developmental Psychotherapy's emphasis on the caregivers as central to treatment success. In addition, I do not want to begin working with the child if the parents are having difficulties that will interfere with their creating a sense of safety in the session. My first one or two sessions are often only with the caregivers. This allows me to develop an alliance with them, discuss parenting issues, begin talking about their family of origin experiences and how these may relate to the current situation, and begin to elaborate on what comprises therapy. Implicitly and explicitly the importance of parenting and parents is discussed. This is not "drive-by" therapy in which the parents drive by, drop off the child, and are not directly involved in treatment. For many families, past experience with treatment has set up an expectation that the therapist will "fix" the child, meet with the child alone, and not share with the parents the content of those sessions. That is not how Dyadic Developmental Psychotherapy proceeds. Parents are central. The therapist acts as coach, director, and supporting actor in the drama that unfolds in the office. Agreement on the frequency of sessions, how long treatment may take, important markers to consider, the role of the therapist, and other issues and recommendations, such as that it may be best for the child to be at home with the parent on a full-time basis, should all be discussed or identified so that later misunderstandings can be avoided. For example, I nearly always discuss with a family in one of our first session something that may occur.

Mom: How should I explain to Henry (eight-year-old son) why we will be coming here?
Therapist: That's a great question. I'm glad you asked it now; thanks. Well, why are we all getting together?
Dad: Because Henry is failing at school, has no friends, and doesn't listen at home.
T: As we talked about during the assessment, these things really bother you both?
D & M: (together) Yes!
T: And would it be fair to say that you both feel that the family could be a happier place than it is?
M: Yes, it's pretty grim now, isn't it, Sam?
D: Yes, not much fun in our home now.

T: So, how would you like your family to be?
M: I'd like us to enjoy each other . . .
D: (Interrupting Mom) And have fun together, like when I grew up.
T: So, why not tell Henry what you just told me? "We are all getting together in therapy to make our family a happier place because no one is having much fun as it is."
M: That simple?
T: Any reason not to?
D: That's good. Henry will get that.
T: Ok, now if that's why we are getting together, I want to ask you both something. If, when we are all together I see something happening or you saying something that I think won't be helpful at that moment, can I interrupt you? Or would that not be OK?
D: (laughing) Sure, just take your shoe off and throw it at me!
M: (laughing) Yes, or toss me a roll of tape.
T: (laughing too) Well, I don't know about that, but would you be insulted or find it disrespectful if I just held out my hand and said, "Hang on a moment;" would that be OK?
M: Sure.
M: OK.

By bringing up this issue of what I will do if I see something happening that is not helpful, later misunderstandings can be avoided. When I do interrupt in some future session, the parents will not feel disrespected or that I was rude. They will know that my intention is to be helpful to them in working toward their goal of having a "happier family."

Developing a treatment contract with a child can be as simple as the parents saying, "We're here so we can be a happier family." Another approach I sometimes use is that I may have the child complete the Sentence Completion Questionnaire. Usually we can pull out several of their responses to use as the basis for a treatment contract.

Therapist: (talking with fourteen-year-old Jenna) I see here that you wrote in response to "Mother and I" that "we fight all the time." Would you like it if you two didn't fight so much? Would that be better for you?
Jenna: She's the one who starts it with all her stupid rules.
Mom: Now . . .
T: (interrupting) Hang on a minute Mrs. Emerson. Jenna, do you think you would be happier if there was less fighting?
Jenna: Yea, I guess.
T: OK, we can work on that. Now what about this one, other children always "make fun of me." Wow, that sounds hard for you. Would you like that different?
J: Well, they are jerks anyway.

T: If there were kids who weren't jerks at school, would you like it if they were nicer?
J: Sure, wouldn't you?
T: You bet I would! Ok, we can work on that one too. Now, what about this one, Father and I "never talk." You and your Dad never talk; would you want to?
J: No, he's always yelling at me, and nothing I do is good enough for him.
T: Hum . . . Well, if that could be different, would you like that?
J: He'll never change.
T: You think he'll never change and stop yelling at you and that nothing you do will ever be good enough for him. That must be so hard for you?
J: (looking at me now) It is. I wish he'd just be happy with me.
T: If that were different, would you like that?
J: Good luck to you, but sure, why not?
T: OK, so we have three things we could work on here. Mom and you not fighting so much, developing some friendships with nicer kids, and being able to talk with your Dad in a way that didn't make you feel bad. Does that sound right?
J: Yeah, so?!
T: Well, those are things we can work on here and maybe even make better. How would that be?
J: Fine, but not when I have basketball practice, and she (pointing to mom) has to come too.
T: Great, so Mrs. Emerson, does that sound OK to you? We'll all work together on these things?
M: I'd like that Jenna, and I'll have Dad come too. I know he'd like this to be different, too and that he feels really bad about how he yells. I feel bad that we fight so much honey. I know I have to get better at this.

Forming Initial Theories

The therapist begins to develop initial guesses regarding the meaning of various events and behaviors. It is very important that the therapist keep an open mind. These are beginning hypotheses, avenues to explore. It is essential that the therapist not focus too early on only one theory as the correct meaning. If the therapist keeps an open mind and views these initial hypotheses as first guesses to be explored, then the therapist will do so in an interested and curious manner and be open to new meanings. If the therapist remembers that the therapist wants to be an ACE therapist, that will help the therapist focus on the tentative nature of initial theories of behavior and events and their associated meanings for the client. It is the meaning for the parent or child that is the primary focus.

Creating a Secure Base

In this phase the therapist is building the foundation for a secure base, which is the primary task of the next phase, Maintaining the Alliance. The therapist begins creating a secure base with PACE and PLACE. Creating a secure base means creating a secure sense of safety and security in the therapy room and at home. A basic tenant of trauma treatment (Briere & Scott, 2006) is "safety first." Without physical, emotional, and psychological safety, which defines the secure base, there cannot be effective treatment. A person under threat is operating with a survival brain, not a learning brain. The therapist begins creating a secure base by enjoying the parent and child. The therapist's constancy, reliability, and consistency help create predictability and safety. Safety is achieved through appropriate structure, consistent with the client's developmental age (Becker-Weidman, 2009). Routines and rituals within the session and at home help create safety.

A secure base is developed by creating concordant intersubjective experiences through the affective/reflective dialogue. The therapist's job is to maintain a healing PACE of treatment. This involves the co-regulation of affect. In this phase, maybe more so than in other phases, there is an emphasis on follow-lead-follow. It is essential to follow the other more than lead the other. Managing the closeness and distance in the relationship is a central task for the therapist in this phase. It helps to know what is the state-of-mind-with-respect-to-attachment of the parent and child. Those with an avoidant or dismissing stance require the therapist to gently increase closeness and reflection. Those with an ambivalent or preoccupied stance require the therapist to concentrate on providing focus, perspective, and structure. Those with a disorganized stance need the therapist to provide containment, organization, meanings, and emotional regulation.

Primary Intervention Strategies

While all the components of Dyadic Developmental Psychotherapy are used in treatment, in this phase the primary intervention strategies or components of Dyadic Developmental Psychotherapy are:

- Creation of concordant intersubjective experiences
- Follow-lead-follow
- PACE
- Co-regulation of affect

Other components that a number of very experienced practitioners of Dyadic Developmental Psychotherapy have described as also having a higher salience are:

- Therapist use of self
- Connections not compliance

The co-regulation of affect is particularly important in this phase because building an alliance requires that the therapist create a safe environment to promote the safe base necessary for exploration. Emotional and psychological safety is created when emotions are present and are not dysregulating. Maintaining connections becomes the therapist's primary focus in this initial phase of treatment. It is a major challenge to maintain an emotionally meaningful connection with a child whose life experience has taught the child to be wary of relationships or to avoid relationships or who finds relationships threatening and frightening. Sometimes parents may want their child to "behave" or "talk" in a session. It is important that in the sessions with only the caregiver that the therapist clarify roles and responsibilities. It is the therapist's responsibility to "manage" the session. The parent can be reassured that the parent does not have to make the child talk or behave. The focus is on building connections. Through the use of the follow-lead-follow component, emphasizing the follow, the therapist can build the connections with parent and child necessary for a secure base in treatment. Following the lead of the client demonstrates a deep acceptance of the child and parent that many have not previously experienced. Neither one is forced to do or say anything at this point or at any other point in treatment. The focus is on building connections. The focus is on creating the alliance.

The end of this phase and the beginning of the next phase is a fluid fuzzy area; no bright white lines here. The therapist will at some point realize that not as much effort and time must be spent in staying connected with the client. The atmosphere is more relaxed, collaborative, and reciprocal. The client is beginning to be less wary, less frightened (fear is often exhibited by a child as defiance, oppositional behavior, and argumentativeness), and easier to engage in discussions generally and in affective/reflective dialogues more specifically. The "lead" portion of follow-lead-follow becomes easier to enter into and can persist for a longer period of time before the therapist has to follow.

MAINTAINING THE ALLIANCE (CREATING THE SECURE BASE)

Now that an alliance is developing, the therapist's focus moves toward maintaining that fragile beginning alliance. The focus in this phase is on deepening and strengthening the alliance so that the difficult task of exploration can begin and expand. This phase may begin as early as the first session with a family or it may take months to create enough of an alliance to be in this phase. This phase overlaps with the other phases. Throughout treatment the therapist must attend to the state of the alliance with the client. Interactive repair plays a key role in the process of maintaining the alliance. There will be inevitable breaches in the relationship. The therapist will make various errors of judgment and timing. All of these disruptions to the alliance must be repaired. Making honest mistakes, mistakes made despite good intentions, do not necessarily create problems in treatment. It is the lack of repair of these mistakes that creates problems in treatment. This is why the therapist's use of self is so important throughout treatment. If the therapist's shame about committing an error leads to the therapist avoiding acknowledging the mistake and working to repair the error, that will cause significant damage to the alliance.

While all of the components of Dyadic Developmental Psychotherapy will be used, five have particular salience at this phase of treatment. These five components are: PACE, intersubjectivity, follow-lead-follow, interactive repair, and the co-regulation of affect. In this second phase of treatment the therapist will want to pay particular attention to using follow-lead-follow as the beginning approach into the exploration phase. How the client responds to the "lead" step of follow-lead-follow is a measure of how quickly and deeply the therapist can move into exploration and a measure of the strength and depth of the alliance. The use of interactive repair is a central element of this phase, which, as previously mentioned, overlaps the other phases. In later phases while less attention is required to maintain the alliance, maintenance of the alliance remains an important part of treatment. As in the previous phase, the therapist will use PACE to create concordant intersubjective experiences, which are a primary means of co-regulating affect and necessary to create and maintain a working alliance.

Primary Tasks

In this second phase the therapist has several primary tasks. The therapist's goal is to develop and expand the secure base for exploration, integration, and healing. The therapist's primary tasks in this second phase are:

- Deepening and strengthening the therapeutic alliance
- Managing emotional proximity
- Exploring initial theories of behavior: the meanings to be explored.
- Repairing relationship breaches.

The primary intervention strategies or components of Dyadic Developmental Psychotherapy that are used in this phase are:

- PACE
- Intersubjectivity

- Follow-lead-follow
- Interactive repair
- Co-regulation of affect

Deepening and Strengthening the Therapeutic Alliance

At the start of this phase there is a beginning secure base. The therapist now can focus on deepening and strengthening the secure base. This is accomplished by focusing on deepening and strengthening the therapeutic alliance. Interactive repair is another necessary component of the process of deepening the therapeutic alliance. In this phase the therapist is attending to strengthening the alliance and secure base so that exploration can occur in an ever deepening manner. The stronger the secure base and alliance, the deeper exploration can go and the stronger the emotions that the relationship can contain. Once the foundation of a secure base has been established in the previous phase, this must be extended, deepened, and further developed. While the phases are presented in a sequential manner, there is substantial overlap among the phases. Exploration of emotionally meaningful and potentially disturbing memories, experiences, and events begins to occur early in treatment in a titrated manner. The secure base of the therapy room and the home are the containers within which exploration occurs. The stronger the container, the deeper the exploration can go without causing dysregulation, which must be avoided.

The alliance and secure base can be strengthened using PACE. By being playful, the therapist creates joyful and enjoyable concordant intersubjective experiences. These mutually shared experiences with shared emotion, attention, and complementary intentions deepen the level of trust and connections between therapist and client. Being playful is also a way to avoid conflicts, arguments, power struggles, and other discordant interchanges. After all, it does take two to have a disagreement. Being accepting of the client's emotions and perspective is also a fine way to avoid power-struggles and maintain an emotionally meaningful alliance. Helping the client experience emotional closeness that is helpful and enjoyable is itself therapeutic.

Sometimes children are familiar with conflictual and emotionally distant relationships and will act in ways to evoke a response from the adults that feels familiar to the child. In this example, eight year old Mara seems to be acting in a way to evoke a critical and emotionally distant alliance.

> Therapist: (to the mom and dad) It sounds like it was so hard for Mara when her aunt and uncle were nice to her older sister and were hurtful to Mara. Maybe Mara felt something was wrong with her and felt bad?

Mara: (screams) Shut up. (Continues for the next twenty seconds yelling) You a f#@*er, you f#@*, you're a s*(%head, you're stupid, you're a loser!!!!
T: (Just before mom and dad appear ready to jump in and tell Mara to stop it, to be nice and stop being disrespectful) (Smiling) Well, that's Dr. Loser to you!
M: (starts laughing), Oh, ok, sure, why not.
Mom & Dad (start laughing)
T: It seems to me, Mara, that must have been so hard for you with your aunt and uncle.
M: I hated it.

So, by accepting what Mara was saying and by being playful, the therapist maintained the alliance which kept the secure base of the therapy in place and allowed beginning exploration to go deeper.

Managing Emotional Proximity

This can be a very challenging task, especially early in treatment when the secure base is barely established, the alliance is fragile, and the client has little experience of the therapist and the relationship. In these circumstances, much of the client's perceptions and interactions with the therapist will be guided by the client's internal working models of past experiences with adults, therapists, and those who purported to be helpful. Clients who have a secure state of mind with respect to attachment will have had positive experiences and largely have resolved negative experiences. Their internal working models will allow them to enter into the treatment relationship in a relatively open, trusting, cooperative, and collaborative manner. The stance of someone with a history of unresolved complex trauma who may have an insecure or disorganized pattern of attachment will be more rigid, suspicious, cautious, and distant. Not surprisingly this may lead to an initial relationship in which suspicion and hesitancy to be open are the dominant themes. The therapist's challenge in these instances is to increase emotional closeness while maintaining the alliance and deepening the secure base. The playful part of PACE can create greater emotional proximity, and these experiences will serve to strengthen the secure base and support deeper exploration.

Exploring Initial Theories of Behavior: The Meanings to Be Explored

Now that the alliance has begun to be solidified and a secure base established, the therapist can begin to explore the initial theories of behavior developed during the assessment and the previous phase. These meanings to be explored are rough guides and should not be viewed as certainties. The therapist must avoid becoming enamored with one's own hypotheses. This can lead to a desire to try to sell the theory or convince the client that the therapist is right. Being flexible and open and tentative in one's investment in the theory allows the therapist to use PACE as it should be used: to accept the other's point of view and openly and with interest and genuine curiosity explore the meanings that may be.

Meanings are explored using the follow-lead-follow and ACE formats. The therapist begins with the client's statement and follows that with acceptance. The judicious use of questions (curiosity) leads the therapist to a deeper understanding of the client's world view and into the client's internal working model. After the therapist has empathized with the client's internal working model, then leading the client can occur. It is very important that the client feel accepted and understood by the therapist before the therapist begins leading the client in a different direction. By creating for the client the experience of being deeply understood and accepted, the therapist strengthens the secure base of treatment, and the client will more willingly follow the therapist in a new direction.

In the following vignette, the therapist is talking with a foster mother early in treatment. They have a beginning relationship; Ms. Kay is understandably cautious. This is the fourth therapist she's been to in the three years she's had Barry, all with no change, help, or even appreciation for how difficult living with Barry can be.

Therapist: Hi, Grace, how's the week been?

Ms. Grace Kay: Awful, you have no idea.

T: What happened? (Accepting and being curious)

G: Barry was a stinker; he lied to me about not doing his homework, and I took his i-Pod, and then he screamed at me so I sent him to his room.

T: (rather than address the punitive quality of the discipline in a lecture, at this early phase of maintaining the alliance, the therapist moves to use ACE and follow-lead-follow to strengthen the alliance and secure base of treatment) That sounds awful; you must have been really upset.

G: What's wrong with him? He's been with me nearly two years and I want to adopt him and he knows it. Why would he lie about his homework? He knows how I feel about lying!

T: It really is odd, isn't it? I mean you care about him and you try to help him with school. What would make him not tell the truth about his homework? What's your guess?

G: He didn't want to get in trouble with me!

T: Oh, what would have happened if he'd told you he'd not done his homework?

G: Nothing, I'd have asked him if he needed help and then I'd help him. He knows that!

T: That's strange. Since he'd not have been in trouble if he'd told you he didn't or couldn't do his homework, what would make him not tell you?
G: I don't know. I can't figure that boy out.
T: Well, if he really believed you were there to help him, wouldn't he come to you?
G: I guess.
T: So, if we look at his behavior as a message to us about how he feels and how he sees relationships, what does his hiding his not doing his homework tell us? (The therapist continues to phrase statements in a joining, "you and me together" sort of way)
G: He must not trust me, but why? It's been almost two years?
T: Ok, that makes sense. Barry doesn't tell you because he doesn't trust you. Maybe he's scared of something bad happening to him, of your doing something bad. Why would he think that?
G: Hmmm. His birth family was really abusive. He came to me with a broken arm and three broken ribs and he's had at least three skull fractures. Maybe he thinks if he doesn't do what I want, like his homework, I'll hurt him like they did.
T: That makes sense. So, what you're telling me is that maybe he was afraid to tell you he couldn't do his home work. Then he had to make up a story to cover that up because he was afraid he'd get hurt?
G: Yes, that could be.
T: OK, so if we follow your theory, and it really makes sense, Grace, then what would be the best approach?
G: Oh my, sending him off and punishing him probably only made him feel worse.

Comment: So, Grace now has a new understanding of her foster-son's behavior and this leads her to a new understanding of how to approach him. The therapist begins using acceptance and follow-lead-follow to develop the alliance further so that exploration of new meanings of Barry's behavior can begin.

Repairing Relationship Breaches

Inevitably there will be breaches in the relationship, and the therapist must repair those. This deepens the alliance and models for the parents what the therapist would like them to do at home with the child. In this phase of treatment, repairing relationship breaches is especially important. The reason for this is "confirmation bias." What this refers to is the psychological process in which one tends to recall events and situations that confirm perceptions, pre-conceived notions, and internal working models while discounting and forgetting things that do not confirm biases. As a result of this process, a parent may, for example, be "nice" 95 percent of the time, and only lose his or her temper "once in a blue moon." The child with complex trauma or a difficult past will remember that one time vividly, and the other times the parent was "nice" will not seem so important and may not come to mind. Hence, the comment often heard, "You never let me do anything." The child remembers the one time the child was told "No" vividly and does not recall with much clarity the 99 other times the child was told "Yes." Past history has taught the child that adults and caregivers are usually hurtful, mean, unhelpful, or uncaring. So interactions that confirm this bias have much more salience than interactions that do not confirm this bias. Therefore, relationship repair is especially important in this phase of treatment. The child may perceive the breach in the relationship in a negative way, confirming the child's experiences of past trauma. Repair of the breach is necessary to begin to expose and change the associated internal working model.

Summary

Maintaining the alliance is a phase that ebbs and flows throughout treatment. Early in treatment it takes on much more importance as the alliance is new and fragile. Later in treatment, when the relationship has more emotional depth, when treatment experiences have clearly demonstrated the therapist's intention to be helpful, and when exploration and healing have led to more flexible and current-reality centered internal working models, this phase becomes less important. It isn't that it is less important to maintain the alliance; it is that the therapist does not need to spend as much time and does not need to focus as much on this because the relationship has enough depth and strength to have some degree of self-regulation and to be self-sustaining.

The primary goals in this phase of deepening and strengthening the therapeutic alliance are achieved by the use of PACE, follow-lead-follow, and an emphasis on interactive repair. These three components of Dyadic Developmental Psychotherapy, along with the others mentioned, will help create the concordant intersubjective experiences that lead to a more secure base and deeper exploration.

EXPLORATION

Once a secure base has begun to be established, exploration can begin. Exploration requires some sense of safety and security. Exploration may begin very early during treatment or even during the assessment, as long as safety (physical, emotional, and psychological) and security are present. As the secure base is deepened, so then can exploration go deeper and healing can begin. While exploration is occurring, the secure base must continue to be maintained and strengthened. In this regard, interactive repair continues to be an important component in this phase. So, while the phases clearly overlap, it is useful to discuss the exploration phase in a discrete manner, so that the therapist can focus on the essential elements of exploration, the middle phase of treatment.

While all of the components of Dyadic Developmental Psychotherapy will be used in this phase and throughout treatment, the primary components of treatment in this phase involve the review of history leading to a healthier and more secure integration. These components include PACE, the creation of concordant intersubjective experiences, the reflective function, insightfulness, follow-lead-follow, interactive repair, commitment, co-creation of meaning, and the co-regulation of affect. Of these, I would focus on the co-creation of meaning and co-regulation of affect as having particular importance. As has been described previously, PACE leads to concordant intersubjectivity. Concordant intersubjectivity, interactive repair, and the reflective function help co-regulate emotions. The affective/reflective dialogue and insightfulness, along with PACE, facilitate the co-creation of meaning.

In this third phase of treatment the therapist will now have helped create a secure base allowing for exploration. As this exploration facilitates integration and the strengthening of the alliance, the therapist can continue to go deeper. While follow-lead-follow continues to be a useful component in this phase, and becomes more significant as more emotionally charged and difficult material is explored, the therapist can move more quickly into the lead element of this component than in previous phases. As material with stronger emotional valence is explored, interactive repair also gains salience.

Primary Tasks

In this third phase the therapist has several primary tasks. The goal is to explore history, memories, events, and experiences that continue to shape the client's relationships and that continue to affect behavior and functioning. Primary tasks in this phase are:

- Exploring how the past is alive in the present
- Exploration of internal working models
- Exploring the meanings of events and behavior.
- Developing the reflective function.

The primary components of Dyadic Developmental Psychotherapy that are used in this phase are:

- Co-creation of meaning
- Co-regulation of affect
- PACE

Other components that are important in this phase are:

- Intersubjectivity (shared emotion, attention, and intention)
- Follow-lead-follow
- Affective/reflective dialogue
- Interactive repair
- Reflective function
- Insightfulness

Uncovering the Past in the Present

Uncovering how the past is alive in the present can be viewed as the major task of this phase of treatment. It encompasses the exploration of internal working models, exploring the meaning of events and behavior, and leading to an enhanced reflective function. Internal working models guide actions and function as a set of unspoken assumptions about relationships, people, caregivers, self, and the world. These internal working models can be thought of as the lenses through which experiences are filtered. If the lenses are clear, there may be little distortion. If there is a notable mismatch between the external world and relationships and the internal working models that guide behavior, and which are the underlying assumptions that evoke emotional states, then we may observe significant difficulties of a psychological, emotional, and behavioral nature. Past experiences and trauma have led to the creation of internal working models that reflect those past relationships and experiences, such as: "You can't rely on adults or others to help;" "Don't trust others; they will hurt you or let you down;" "Adults mostly do bad things to me;" "I am bad;" "I am not wanted, I am unlovable, and I am not valued;" "Don't try, nothing matters;" and so forth. These negative internal working models lead to emotional states and resultant behaviors that reflect these core beliefs. In many ways these internal working models can lead to behavior that was quite adaptive in the original setting, but which is highly dysfunctional in the new setting. For example, hoarding food and objects may be quite adaptive and helpful in an orphanage or in a neglectful home. Taking what is needed makes sense if in the child's world the child cannot rely on the caregivers to provide what is needed. In the new setting, that may be called "stealing." Behaviors that were adaptive become dysfunctional if the setting changes. The child who has experienced significant relational trauma, and whose survival brain is largely active will have a very difficult time learning new ways of relating and recognizing the new circumstances in an emotionally meaningful way. These children exhibit a rigidity that comes from the lack of a secure base. Without a secure base, exploration is not possible. Without exploration, recognizing new experiences and changing behavior is not possible. So, exploration of the internal working models and how the past is alive in the present is the primary task of this phase.

Exploration of internal working models and of the meaning of events, behaviors, and intentions relies on several components of Dyadic Developmental Psychotherapy. PACE provides the framework within which the therapist works with the family. Pacing is important so that dysregulation is avoided. The ACE therapist, using follow-lead-follow, creates concordant intersubjective experiences that engage the client where the client is at that moment and then leads the client deeper into memories and emotionally meaningful experiences with parents and with the therapist. In this phase of treatment the therapist will find that the initial "follow" portion of follow-lead-follow can be relatively brief, primarily because the secure base creates a sense of safety and security that allows trust to flourish. This also co-regulates client affect. The creation of concordant intersubjective experiences within the therapy setting is one element of co-regulating emotions. Another component that may be needed is interactive repair. Especially when the therapist makes a mistake, it will be important to repair the relationship and reconstitute the secure base. Helping parents with interactive repair will facilitate deeper exploration at this point in treatment.

The co-creation of meaning is a central component of this phase. The affective/reflective dialogue is also a major component in this phase. Exploration requires that the dialogue have both elements, emotion and reflection. Increasing reflective abilities and insightfulness lead to better affect regulation. Exploration leads to a making explicit the internal working models, which allows for the creation of new meanings that reflect both the past and the present. The new meanings reflect an integration of past events, relationships, and history with new circumstances, new relationships, and functioning at a new developmental phase. For example, the meaning the child ascribed to events when the child was five years old and being beaten will be different today as a result of exploration and the co-creation of new meanings. At age five the child may have developed an understanding of self that the child was bad, that the abuse was the child's fault, and that loud voices meant abuse is coming. At age five the child was alone and had to make sense of the world through the eyes of a frightened five year old whose survival brain was operating. At age ten, in a caring and committed family, a new meaning can be co-created by the child, parents, and therapist. As the experiences are revisited within the safety created in the therapist's office, with the parents (rather than alone), and with the learning brain being more operative, the ten year old can develop a new and more functional meaning of these events. As a result of this exploration at a more advanced developmental stage, making explicit the negative internal working model, and through the relationship, a new meaning can be co-created, and the internal working model is changed.

Two examples will illustrate how the past, as it is alive in the present, is explored and how new meanings evolve. In the first example, I am talking with twelve-year old Erik. Erik was adopted at age ten by the Smiths. Erik had lived with a neglectful drug-addicted mother and three older siblings, two of whom had been abusive to Erik. The oldest sibling, Rhonda, had been a sort of surrogate mother to the children. When Erik's mother died of a drug overdose, the children were placed in foster care, and after a year Erik was placed with the Smiths. Erik was a bright child who showed a mix of very immature behavior and very pseudo-independent functioning. His immaturity was often perceived as "cute" by teachers and other adults. This behavior was a response to living in chronically threatening home. The survival brain has four basic response patterns: fight, flight, freeze, or appeasement. Erik's response was appeasement. Erik's seemingly independent behavior can be understood as an adaptive response to a neglectful world, "If I don't take care of myself, no one will." This led to his new parents perceiving Erik as "controlling," because he'd always have to do things "his" way and he never wanted their help. The following exchange took place about twelve sessions into treatment. I greeted the family in the waiting room and asked them to come back to my office. This meeting took place on a winter evening. Mr. and Mrs. Smith had hung up their jackets and got up to come back to my office. Erik picked up his large and very full backpack (he'd come from school), the books he was working on, along with his jacket, boots, his soda and a bag of food from a local fast food restaurant, and with all this precariously balanced, walked with his parents to my office. As they sat down on the couch the following interchange occurred.

Therapist: Wow, Erik, that's a lot of stuff. (Beginning with what is happening right now and accepting what is there, and following, from follow-lead-follow)
Erik: (smiling) Yeah.
T: Hey, you know what I was thinking? (Now on to lead. I ask a question and in this manner engage him as I lead him to explore the meaning of this event)
E: No, what?
T: I was thinking that I bet it didn't even cross your mind to ask anyone to help you with all that.
E: (eyes widen and he appears and sounds threatened/scared/blamed/criticized) No, no, it didn't!

T: (repairing relationship) Oh, I know. I'm not criticizing you. I was just noticing that you sure had a lot of stuff there and that I bet it never even occurred to you to ask your mom or dad or me to help carry any of that stuff.
E: No, it didn't.
T: That reminds me of something; can I tell you?
E: Sure
T: (I want to reengage Erik and his parents and go a bit deeper, so I decide to "tell a story," which usually captures everyone's attention and also serves to get everyone thinking along the same path, which is one crucial element of concordant intersubjectivity.) Well, my son can't really see red or green. You know what that's called?
E: No, what?
T: Let's see if your parents know, ask them.
E: Mom, what is that called?
Mrs. Smith: He's color blind, right?
T: Yes! Exactly! My son is color blind. He has trouble seeing red and green. Pink shirts look white to him. He's learned over time to compensate for that. For example, he puts a mark on his pink shirts on the collar tag. When he was learning to drive he had to learn to stop when the top light was lit and go when the bottom light was lit.
Mr. Smith: My uncle was color blind.
T: Really? Could you tell he was?
Mr. S: No, I only know because he told us once.
T: Well, you know what, Erik?
E: What?
T: (we begin an affective/reflective dialogue here) I was remembering that when you were with your first family, you didn't have many people around you could rely on for help. Am I remembering that right?
E: Yes, Mom was great when she was there and not stoned, but she got stoned a lot. My two sisters were always mean to me, and Bobby, my older brother, sometimes helped me, but he wasn't around a lot.
T: What was that like for you?
E: I was scared a lot.
T: That must have been so hard to be alone like that and scared a lot.
E: Yes, it was.
T: Do your parents know this? How hard it was for you? Maybe you could tell them that?
E: (looks at Mom) It was really hard for me being scared all the time.
Mom: I am so sorry Erik, I wish I could have been there to help you.
E: Yeah, me too!
T: So you didn't have much help around when you were younger. That might make it really hard to know what help is like and when it might be available.
E: I guess.
T: Just like my son can't see certain colors, I think you don't see help even when it is right in front of you. My son's color blind and you're help-blind!

(This is the new meaning for Erik's behavior. Not that he's "too independent" or "doesn't trust us," or "controlling"; it is that he's help-blind).
Mrs.: I never thought of that!
T: Do you know what I mean, Erik?
E: Yeah, you mean I can't see help when it's available?
T: (In an excited slightly louder tone) Yes! Exactly! That's right. What was it like carrying all that stuff in here?
E: It was hard!
T: It sure looked hard to carry all that stuff. And it never even crossed your mind to ask anyone here for help did it?
E: No, I never even thought of doing that.
T: What do you think your mom or dad would have done if you'd asked them to help carry some of that stuff?
E: Umm, I don't know.
T: I'm so glad you said that Erik, I think that's so true, you're not sure what they'd say or do. When you're help blind it's hard to see that help could be there. Why don't you ask them what they'd do?
E: Dad, what would you have done if I'd asked you to carry something?
Mr.: I'd have helped you, Son. I'd have picked up some of your books and stuff. I like helping you. That's what dads do.
T: (to the parents) Does this make sense to you two that Erik is "help-blind?" That he just doesn't see help when it is there. So, he'll need your help for him to see help.
Mrs.: It makes so much sense.

In this example, we see exploration occurring and the co-creation of meaning, and the integration of past events into current circumstances to build a new meaning for the behavior. The affective/reflective dialogue that precedes the creation of the new meaning adds emotional valence that makes the new meaning more significant.

The second example occurred in the first session with a family and illustrates that these phases overlap and can occur in a quickly evolving sequence. Joseph lived with his three birth brothers and his adoptive parents. Joseph was the youngest. Joseph was removed from his birth mother from the hospital and placed in foster care for two years before moving into the Jones' home with his brothers. In the first part of this first session, I'd met with the parents alone for about half an hour. The following is from that session:

Margaret: He gets so argumentative when me or Mitch suggest anything.
Therapist: I wonder what would make him get so angry and, as you've described it, defiant? (I am trying to expand their view and develop their insightfulness into Joe's behavior)
Mitch: Maybe he just likes to argue
T: (accepting that) OK, what would make him want to argue?

Mitch: I don't know; that's why we're here.
T: Well, the two of you may have some guesses.
Margaret: I think he just argues with us, but then later when he's had a chance to think about it, he does come back and will talk with us and even accept our ideas.
T: So, you're trying to help him, trying to be helpful, and he is sort of fighting you.
Marg: Yes.
T: It's almost like he must perceive what you are doing as a bad thing or a hurtful thing. I mean the way he reacts doesn't look like he sees what you are doing as trying to be helpful.
Marg: No, we're not arguing with him or trying to get into a fight. (Both Margaret and Mitch have a difficult time seeing how Joseph may experience the world so differently than they do.)
T: You're trying to be helpful, right?
Marg: Yes
T: So maybe it's like "telephone." The message sent, that you want to help him, isn't the message received. Maybe he hears something different.
Mitch: I don't know. I've had several discussions with him that we don't like his arguing and his defiance and that we're trying to help him. He seems to get it, but then he starts all over again.
T: It is confusing
Mitch: He just doesn't get it.
T: Maybe his view of the relationship or the dialogue is different than yours. I say that because his reaction is so different that what you each think it should be.
Marg: Yes, it is.

Comment: I don't seem to be able to connect with the parents and help them see what I see, so I drop this topic and we talk about how Joseph (Joe) is doing in school and a few other things. This is an example of therapist use of self, the importance of the therapist's reflective capabilities, and of the therapist not becoming too firmly wedded to one idea. By remaining flexible and maintaining a continuous state of awareness of the ebb and flow of emotions and process in the session and my impact on this, I am able to act in a therapeutic manner and avoid merely lecturing or arguing. I focus instead on developing and maintaining a secure base with the parents by focusing on PACE and giving them a lot of empathy about how hard they are trying and how difficult it's been these past thirteen years. Then I go get Joe to join us. About fifteen minutes into the session with Joseph, age fifteen, we had the following interchange.

Therapist: Hi, Joe, how are you?
Joe: Fine.

T: (To Dad; Joe is sitting between Mom and Dad on the couch) Is he as tall as you? (I begin by noticing something about the family to begin our talk)
Dad: (Joe sits up now) Taller, see?
Mom: He's way taller than me.
Dad: Yep, he's tall and lanky (Joe has a puzzled look on his face).
Joe: I'm not lanky
Dad: Do you know what lanky means?
Joe: No.
Dad: It means tall and thin.
T: What made you say that you're not lanky if you didn't know what it means? (Curious about his response and what is underneath it)
J: You should always say "No" to a question in school.
T: (Eyes wide, in a playful tone) Always? Like if a teacher asks you if you have a hall pass, and you do. You should say no?
J: No, but to any question when you don't know the word, say "No."
Mom: Why?
J: Because whenever you get asked a question, it's bad.
T: So your default position is "NO!" (I lead Joe a bit deeper here)
J: Right, because it'll be bad.
T: Oh, so, like when your mom or dad asks you something, it's gonna be bad, so "No" is sort of your default position? (Now I lead the discussion deeper to explore how his internal working model may affect his experience of his parents)
J: Yeah.
T: (to parents) So Joe's default position seems to be that questions mean something bad is in the works. That's sort of what we were talking about earlier before Joe came in. (In this interchange I want to connect our previous discussion to what is happening here and now)
Dad: What do you mean?
T: Oh, when we were talking before Joe came in about how your intentions when you ask Joe something are to be helpful but that usually an argument develops, so it seemed like you mean to be helpful but maybe Joe perceives your intentions differently: his default is that something bad is going to happen.
D: Oh, yeah, right.
T: (to Joe) Do you know what we are saying?
J: No.
T: Maybe your parents could explain it. Who do you want to ask?
J: I don't care.
T: OK, so who will you ask?
J: Ummm, both (then turns to Dad). Can you explain it?
D: What we're saying Joe is that when we ask about your day or ask you to do something, we mean to help you.
J: Whenever we sit at the table for a discussion, you are criticizing me. I know if we sit at the table, I'm in trouble.

D: We want to help you, and you don't see that. You think that you are in trouble.
J: Oh, now I get it.
T: So somehow your parents have good intentions, and you don't see it that way.
J: No, I don't.
T: Wow, that must be so hard for you, Joe, to often think your parents don't have good intentions toward you. No wonder you and your parents argue so much. They think they are trying to be helpful and you don't feel they are and then say "NO!" and then they push on, and you get more annoyed, and they get more annoyed.
J: It's not fun.
T: So, would that be something you'd all like, to be a happier family and not argue as much?
Mom, Dad, Joe: (At the same time) Yes!

At the end of this session I meet briefly with the parents to discuss the session and the following interchange occurred:

Therapist: So, what did you think of the session?
Dad: I'll have to change how I talk to Joseph.
T: What do you mean?
D: If he's not getting what I mean I'll just have to try to get it across better.
T: Oh, you mean like if maybe you were more explicit about what is your intention. Saying something like, "Joe, I have an idea here that I think may be helpful, can I tell you?" Or, "Joe, I want to ask you something so we can figure this out together."
D: (laughing) That's good, yes. Can you write that down for me? (We all chuckle at that.)

Initially the parents did not seem to understand what I was attempting to explain, a new meaning for Joe's behavior. It may have been that because this was our first session together we just did not have enough of a secure base in place for that sort of exploration to occur so that my attempt was premature. In the session, while maintaining concordant intersubjectivity among all family members and using a follow-lead-follow format within the PACE framework, the family experienced, rather than intellectually heard, Joe's misperception. The affective/reflective dialogue that ensued enabled the family to experience the interaction, reflect on the interaction, and then develop a new meaning. The new meaning was that Joe was not arguing to argue or to be defiant; he was trying to protect himself and trying to avoid being in trouble.

Interchanges such as those above that rely on memory of past experiences are one way to engage in exploration. Other means can include reviewing past history by reading documents, by role-playing and psychodramatic re-enactments, and by the therapist talking for the child or parent.

Reading Documents

Protective service reports and police reports can provide vivid and detailed descriptions of events and circumstances. The judicious use of these documents within an affective/reflective dialogue can enhance exploration, deepen the client's insight, and aid in the creation of new meanings. The purpose is not to merely read the material and impart the cognitive understanding. The purpose is to create and deepen an affective/reflective dialogue with the client. There is an ebb and flow to this process. The therapist may read a line or two and then pause to explore what that means to the child and the parents and their emotional experience. Exploring the emotions, thoughts, and meanings evoked is the purpose of reading this material.

An example may help illustrate this process. Kara, age ten, has been with her foster mother for two years and will be adopted in the near future. Kara was with her birth family until she was six years old and then was placed in five different foster homes before coming to Ms. Colten's home. Kara has a few fuzzy memories of life with her birth family. She vaguely remembers being alone in her room, being hungry, and hiding in a closet during instances of domestic violence.

Therapist: I have some reports here that I thought we might look at today, if you want.
Kara: What is that?
T: These are papers about when you lived with Tara and Bill (her birth parents, whom she refers to by those names). I thought maybe I'd read some of this to you and your mom.
K: Why do you have those pages folded over?
T: Oh, these (pointing to the folded corners)? I marked the sections of these papers that are about what it was like with Tara and Bill so I could read those to you and we could talk about them.
K: You did that?
T: Yes. Can you guess what made me do that? (Comment: I ask this question to see if she can reflect on my state of mind. In addition, by asking this question, I lead her into an affective/reflective dialogue about intentions.)
K: I don't know
T: I know you don't know. So can you guess?
K: To mark the good parts?
T: Great guess Kara! I marked these parts so that I could find the parts that would be about your birth family and that I thought might be most helpful for us to read. Is that OK; do you want me to read this to you and your mom?

K: Yes.
T: OK, (reading now from a county protective services report):
"On September 19, 2001 the department received a call stating that Kara's mother was being abused by her boyfriend. The caller reported that the boyfriend and mother would both become drunk and then become violent toward each other and the children. A St. Francis county Children and Youth worker and sheriff made an unannounced visit to the apartment and found the apartment strewn with rotting food, animal feces, and dirty dishes. The children were filthy, and Kara's diaper was so old that the worker had to soak it in water to remove it."
T: (moving to reflection) Kara, I wonder what you think of this; how you are feeling now?
K: Why did she do that? Why didn't she change my diaper?
T: You sound really sad. That must have been so hard for you (empathy).
K: (in a very small voice) Yes.
T: (noticing the foster mother's tears) Kara, what do you think your mom's tears are about? (Comment: I initiate a reflective dialogue between Kara and her mother.)
K: (looks at her foster mother with a puzzled look) I don't know.
T: Ask her
K: Mom, why are you crying?
Ms. Colten: I feel so sad for you honey. I wish I could have been there for you and protected you from that. (Noticing that now Kara is crying.) Come here honey. (They hug and cry together.) Now I see why you get so angry when our dog has an accident in the living room. I thought you were being mean to Missy, but now I see you were scared. (Mom's new insight and new meaning will allow her to respond differently and will allow Kara to better understand herself.)

By reading an emotion-laden section of the report that is evocative, mother and child share a deeply moving shared experience together (concordant intersubjectivity). Kara is not alone and can feel cared for and loved by her foster mother. The foster mother's sharing of Kara's pain allows Kara to more deeply experience and share her sadness; this is the power of shared concordant intersubjectivity to deepen experiences. The affective/reflective dialogue that ensues further develops both the parent's and the child's reflective function.

Talking For, Talking About

Another means of deepening an experience and evoking emotion during exploration is for the therapist to talk for or about the child or parent when the client cannot put into words what the client is experiencing. In the previous example with Joe and his parents when Joe said "No" to all questions, I was talking about him in front of Joe with his parents. This allowed him to hear the meaning I was ascribing to the experience without having to directly respond, although he did jump in quickly, which allowed the affective/reflective dialogue to return to a "talking with" format. An example of "talking for" occurred in another session with Joe. The family is seated on the couch together.

Therapist: It sounds like you were really worried about what your Mom and Dad would do if they found out about your being suspended from school. Can you tell them that?
Joe: (looking down at his shoes) No.
Therapist: Could I tell them for you?
Joe: Sure
T: OK, if I get anything wrong, will you correct me?
Joe: Sure
T: OK, so I'll be you, Joe. Mom, Dad, sometimes I don't tell you things like the other day when I got suspended because I get scared that you'll be mad at me. (In an aside to Joe in a stage whisper: "Did I get that right?" Joe nods his head, "Yes," so I go on.) And I get scared that if you get mad at me you won't want me anymore. Are you mad at me?
Mom: Joe, I'm not happy you got suspended for throwing your book at the teacher, but I'm not angry at you. I know school is hard for you and that it's a really long day for you. That's why we want to get you in to another class to help you.
T: (as Joe) See, yes, you are mad at me and you're gonna get rid of me, aren't you?! That special class means I'll have to leave and go to a treatment center to live. (To Joe in a stage whisper, "Is that about right?" Joe: "Yes.")
Mom: Oh, Joe, I am not angry with you. I feel sad that school is so frustrating for you, and I feel angry that no one ever recognized that you have trouble reading and need help with that and other things. I know that the new class is in a school that is part of a residential treatment center, but they take day students and that's what you'll be. We'd never get rid of you; you're my son forever.
Dad: Of course. I'm sorry. I guess when Mom and I were discussing the new class we should have known you'd hear us and I guess you just jumped to a conclusion that you were going there to live.
Joe: Yes, I thought that's why you and Mom where talking about it on the back porch, so I wouldn't know what you had planned for me to get rid of me if I got in trouble one more time.
Dad: I'm sorry; I wish you'd come to us sooner. I guess we should know by now, you have radar ears.
Joe: (laughs) I know everything!

So in this example, I begin by talking for Joe; by saying what I think he may be feeling and thinking. I try to put into words what his experience may be. By frequently checking in with him I keep him involved and make sure I don't stray too far from what is his experience. As often happens, once the dialogue gets going, the child jumps and takes over. If the therapist is reasonably accurate in reflecting the child's experience, it is as if the child actually says the words.

What are the differences between talking about and talking for? Broadly speaking, talking for the child tends to increase the affect and deepen the emotional experience for both the child and the caregiver. Talking about the child, with the child present, tends to decrease the affect. The therapist may want to use talking for the child when the therapist wants to amplify what the child is experiencing. The therapist may consider using talking about the child when the child is experiencing too much affect and the therapist wants to dampen this to avoid dysregulation. Consider the following example of the therapist talking about the child.

Emily is thirteen years old. She has been with the Perigreen family for four years. Before that Emily was in a series of foster homes and residential placements after having been removed from her birth family at six years old because of neglect and severe physical and sexual abuse. This excerpt occurred in a session in which the parents had been talking with Emily about her having gone into their son's room (age ten) and climbed into bed with him in the middle of the night.

Therapist: Emily, you look and sound upset; can you tell me what you are upset about?
Emily: (screams) SHUT UP!!! DON'T TALK!! (covering her ears)
T: (to Sarina Perigreen) Emily is really upset.
Billy: Well, we were pretty upset too when we found her in Billy Jr.'s room!
Emily: I DON'T WANT TO TALK.
T: That's OK Emily; you don't have to say a word. Is it OK if I just talk with your folks?
Emily: (Sullenly) Fine, just don't say anything to me or I'll get up and kick you in the head.
T: (to Billy) Emily is really upset and so are you.
B: Yes, I don't know what she was thinking.
T: Maybe she didn't either. My sense of your daughter is that she sometimes is sort of driven by impulses that she really doesn't understand.
Sarina: When I asked her why, she said, "I don't know."
T: Do you think she really didn't know?
S: Oh, yes, I'm sure she didn't.
E: (looking up now and pulling her hands off her ears, she says in a soft whisper) I didn't, Mom.

S: I know honey. This is really hard for us all. Dad and I got scared. We'll work this out together, OK honey?
E: I guess.
B: I'm sorry I yelled at you, Emily.
E: (looks at Dad through her bangs) Really?
B: Yes, Em. I know this is hard for you.
T: Look at what you've all done here. You are all really working hard at this. I know you (to Emily) sometimes do things that you later regret and that you don't understand. Maybe you even get scared about what your parents will do?
E: I thought they'd send me away.
S: Oh, honey, we'd never send you away. We just gotta help you.
E: OK Mom.

Role-playing & Psychodramatic Re-enactments

Role-playing and psychodramatic re-enactments of specific memories and experiences are another way to deepen the experience and further exploration. In addition, these experiences can lead to significant integration. Role-playing and psychodramatic re-enactments can be used toward the end of this phase and are a part of the next phase, integration. These experiences lead to integration by reworking the experience with parents. Unlike the "first" time the child had the experience and was alone, this time the child has a caregiver present. Not being alone, sharing the emotions of the experience, and doing so in a safe setting, all facilitate integration of the experience and the co-creation of a more advanced understanding and meaning of the experience.

Rose, age six, and her foster mother, Jane, had been together for about two and a half years. Rose had been abused by her birth mother and had vivid memories of her birth mother slamming her against the wall and other violent episodes. Rose herself was aggressive toward Jane. The role-play that follows had been done several times before, and Rose would sometimes ask that we repeat it. Like a favorite bed-time story, the role-play provided her some comfort because she felt safe with Jane. The person playing Rose's birth mother, Sage, tries to act like Sage and use words and phrases Sage used as a way to revisit the trauma to some degree and to evoke affect. It is important for the therapist to gradually increase the intensity; we want some affect present but we never want to dysregulate the child or parent. In playing the character in the role-play it is useful to remember that there are several very important differences between the role-play or psychodramatic re-enactment and the actual experience. First, this time the child is not alone; the child is with an attuned, sensitive, and protective caregiver. Second, the child is developmentally and chronologically older. Third, the intensity is much less than it was during the actual experience in the past. After the role-play, the therapist talks with the family about the experience. This is can be understood as part of the affective/reflective dialogue, an emotional experience followed by reflection.

Jane and Rose enter. Jane sits on the couch and gently pulls Rose onto her lap.
Rose: (to Art) Put on, put a blanket on you and you pretend you're Mommy Jane.
Jane: You mean Mommy Sage?
Rose: Yeah.
Art: You mean Mommy *Sage?*
Jane: Mommy Sage.
Rose: Can you play Mommy Sage?
Art: We could do that. Now who *was* Mommy Sage?
Jane: (Wrapping her arms around Rose) Who was . . . you've got to answer the questions if you want to play the game.
Art: Who *was* Mommy Sage?
Rose: You?
Art. Yeah, but who was she?
Rose: She was a bad, (slight catch in her voice) bad mommy.
Art: Oh, she was a bad mommy?
Rose: (quietly) Yeah.
Art: She was your first mommy, right?
Rose: (Curls up into Jane's arms, subdued, turning away from Art) Yeah.
Art. You lived with her first.
Rose: Yeah.
Art: Want me to pretend I'm Mommy Sage?
Rose: (Buries her face in Jane's shoulder) Yeah.
Art: And what do you want to do? What do you want to say to Mommy Sage?
Rose: (Looks at Art, holding onto Jane's sweater) No! I don't want you, Mommy Sage!
Art: Oh is that it? Okay . . .
Rose: Yeah.
Art: You want me to pretend I'm Mommy Sage?
Rose: Yeah.
Art: Okay, I'll go pretend I'm Mommy Sage.
Rose: Um, just put a blanket on you, alright?
Art: Yeah, I remember that.
(Art exits. I go out of the room to get a blanket to drape over me as I play Sage.)
Jane: What do you want to say to Mommy Sage?
Rose: No, I don't want you.
Jane: Hmmm?
Rose: (Buries face in Jane) I don't want you.
Jane: Hmmmm?
Jane: What if she says (whisper) "Come with me?"
Rose: I won't.

Jane: Hmmm?
Rose: No, I won't come with you.
Jane: You going to tell her no?
Rose: I'll tell her no.
Jane: What if she says . . .
Rose: (loudly) Come with me or you get a spanking!
Jane: What are you going to say?
Rose: No!
Rose: Uh-oh, Mommy Sage is coming.
Jane: Uh-oh.
Rose: Hide me! Hide me! Hide me!
Jane: No. *You* gotta talk to her. *You* told her to come.

Art re-enters, wrapped in a white blanket. He pulls up a chair in front of Jane and Rose and sits facing them.

Art as Mommy Sage: Rose! *My* little girl! Rose, *my* little girl. Oh, I'm so glad to see *you*. You're going to come home with *me*.
Rose: (yells) No. (Curls up closer to Jane turning her face away from Sage into Jane's shoulder)
Sage: Yeah, you're going to come home with me because you're *my* little girl.
Rose: (Looks at Sage with a stern face) NO! I'm *her* little girl. (Curls up closer to Jane and looks at her.)
Sage: You're *her* little girl?
Rose: Yeah.
Sage: Nooo. You're *my* little girl.
Rose: (Peeking at Sage over shoulder) I'm *her* little girl.
Sage: I was your first mommy.
Rose: No, you *weren't*.
Sage: I *was*.
Rose: (louder) No, you *weren't!*
Sage: You came out of my tummy.
Rose: (louder still) NO, I *didn't*.
Sage: You did.
Rose: No, I didn't.
Sage: Whose tummy did you come out of?
Rose: (Looks into Jane's eyes) Her tummy . . . ?
Jane: Who's *her*?
Rose: You.

Jane smiles at Rose and they share a moment together in each others arms.

Sage: Oh, I bet you wish that were true, but you came out of my tummy. (Shaking his finger at Rose) You're my little girl.
Rose: (Raising her voice) No, I'm not!

Sage: You were born to *me,* and I want you! I want you back!
Rose: No, you won't.
Sage: Yeah, you can't have her, Jane! (Rose hugs Jane and pushes her feet under Jane's leg, while Jane tucks in Rose's feet) She's *my* little girl!
Sage: If you don't come . . .
Jane: (Jane hugs Rose to her and Rose tightens her arms around Jane's neck, peeking over at Sage) (loudly) She's *mine*.
Rose: I'm hers.
Sage: I'll bang you against the wall . . . (This is what Sage did to Rose that led to Rose being removed from Sage's home. At this point in the role-play I increase the intensity based on Rose's deeper involvement and on the strength of her voice and posture that reflect her ability to manage these strong feelings with her mom, Jane.)
Rose: (to Jane, looking into her eyes) Say "No!"
Jane: (very loudly) NO!
Sage: You listen to me.
Rose: (whispers to Jane) Say "No."
Jane: (To Rose) *You* tell her.
Rose: (turning to Sage and in loud firm voice says) No!
Sage: You're a *bad* little girl. You listen to me. (This was a phrase that Sage often used in relation to Rose.)
Rose: No!
Sage: You're a bad little girl.
Rose: No!
Sage: Yes, you are!
Rose: Go back, go back home where you come from.
Sage: You *are* a bad little girl!
Rose: Go back where you come from.
Jane: (Whispers to Rose) You tell her you're not a bad girl!
Rose: I'm not a little bad little girl.
Sage: (loudly) Yes, you are!
Rose: (angrily and loudly) No, I'm not!
Sage: You don't listen . . .
Rose: NO! I'm not!
Sage: You don't listen and you're a bad little girl.
Rose: (very loudly) NO, I'M NOT!
Sage: That's why I had to hit you and that's why I had to break that TV . . . because you're a bad little girl.
Rose: (watching intently, she sticks out her tongue at Mommy Sage.)
Sage: (sternly) Don't you stick out your tongue at *me*!
Rose: (Turning to look at Jane, gives a little smile)
Jane: (whispers to Rose) You're not a bad girl you're a good girl! (and hugs Rose).
Rose: (turns to Sage) I'm not bad!

Sage: You're not? (At this point I accept what Jane and Rose are saying and change my approach)
Rose: (shaking her head confidently) Uh uh.
Sage: Uh-uh? You wouldn't listen . . .
Rose: I would!
Sage: (pointing to Jane) You're not going to listen to *her*! She doesn't know how bad you are. (to Jane) You don't know how bad this little girl is. (Jane hugs Rose and Rose hugs Jane.) She's a bad little girl.
Rose: I'm not . . .
Jane: Say "I'm not bad!"
Rose: I'M NOT BAD!
Jane: (whispers to Rose) You tell her. . . . You can't hurt me no more!
Rose: You can't hurt me anymore!
Sage: You're my little girl. I can do whatever I want. (To Jane) You can't have her . . .
Rose: I can karate kick! I can karate kick! I can do karate.
Sage: Yeah, but I'm bigger than you and I'm your mommy. . . . She's not your mommy!
Rose: (whispers to Jane) I can do karate kicks. (Jane smiles as they gaze into each other's eyes)
Jane: Mmm. (whispers to Rose) Tell her I'm your mommy. Tell her!
Sage: (reaching out toward Rose) You're my little girl. I can take you whenever I want!
Rose: (Frowning and tapping her finger on Jane's head she says in a loud and proud voice) She's my mommy!
Sage: She is? (As Sage, I become more uncertain and tentative as Rose's strength and certainty are evident.)
Rose: Yeah.
Sage: No, *I'm* your mommy.
Rose: She won't let you hurt me.
Sage: Yeah, she doesn't know. You don't know, Jane, what she's like. I'm gonna take her! You can't have her. I'm going to take her. She's my little girl . . . you can't have her!
Jane: (holding Rose closely to herself) Oh no, we're going to keep her safe! (to Rose) Huh! You're my little girl!
Rose: (softly) Yeah.

Rose and Jane have each claimed the other and the role-play is largely resolved. Jane has protected Rose, and Rose, feeling safe and secure, is able to directly express herself. It is now time for Sage to leave.

Sage: You can't make me go away, Rose.
Jane: (whispers to Rose) Tell her to go.
Rose: (listens, then yells) Go away!

Sage: You can't make me go away!
Rose: (yells loudly) GO A-WAY!
Sage: You can't . . . I'm your mommy—I'll stay here as long as I want!
Rose: Go A-WAY!
Sage: You can't make me.
Rose: (Rose whispers into Jane's ear) Tell her to go away. (Rose enlists her mom's help to make Sage go.)
Jane: Go away!
Sage: She's mine!
Jane: (hugging Rose more closely) She doesn't want you. Go away!
Sage: She's *my* little girl.
Jane: She's *my* little girl. (Rose gives a smile and a hug. Now that Jane has clearly claimed her daughter, protected her, and wants Sage to leave, I leave.)
Sage: *Fine!* You can have her. I'm leaving! (Sage gets up from the chair and leaves the room, closing the door behind her.)
Rose: (turns and looks in Jane's eyes)
Jane: (smiling and looking into Rose's eyes) We made her go away, didn't we! We BEAT her! Did we beat her?
Rose: (softly) Yeah.
Jane: Did we make her go away?
Rose: Yeah.
Jane: Do you feel better?
Rose: Yes.

The Debriefing

In this reflective part following the role-play, we discuss and reflect on the experience. The role-play is the affective part of this affective/reflective experience, and the debriefing is the reflective component. What the reader will notice is that for Rose, as for all the children I've done role-play's with, it is as if the birth parent was actually present, not someone pretending to be the birth parent.

(Art re-enters)
Art: Rose, who was that lady I saw leaving? I saw some lady leaving. Who *was* she?
Rose: She was . . . she was . . . Mommy Sage. (Notice that Rose does not say, "Silly, that was you," or anything like that. In my experience when children reflect on the role-play either right after or even months later, it is as if the birth parent actually were there.)
Art: That was Mommy Sage!? What was she doing here?
Rose: She was <unintelligible> me.
Art: She was trying to hold you?
Rose: (correcting me) *Hurt* me.

Art: She was trying to hurt you?
Rose: Yeah.
Art: (leaning forward) And then what happened?
Rose: (smiling happily and pointing at Jane) She made her go away.
Art: *She did?*
Rose: Yeah!
Art: Boy, that's good! Whew! She really was trying to hurt you? (Rose hugs Jane more tightly, putting her cheek against Jane's.) Boy! Do you think she would have hurt you?
Art gets up and crosses the room to open the window as he asks the question.
Rose: (relaxing, smiles, following Art's movements with her eyes) Let's play it again! Let's play it again!
Art: You like to play it again? You like to tell her to leave and go?
Rose: Yeah! Can we play again?
Jane: (laughs. To Art) She's getting forceful now! (to Rose) Maybe next time!
Art: (to Rose) Who makes her go?
Rose: (tapping her finger on Jane's head) She and me.
Rose: (smiling) Please, can I play again?
Art: What do you want . . . what do you want . . . I think I can go catch her and have her come back again, but this time maybe there are things you'd like to ask or say to her.
Rose: (looks thoughtful)
Jane: What would you like to ask her?
Rose: (tentatively) Go away?
Jane: (puts her arms around Rose and gives her a big hug)

Commentary: At this point I think that we can do something we've not done before. Something I call the "magic wand." You will read about this integrative experience and how it unfolds with Rose and Jane in the next section on the Integration phase.

An important caveat is that with such a powerful intervention the therapist must take care to co-regulate the participants and avoid dysregulation. The therapist needs some confidence in the parent's capacity to support the child and create safety. The therapist also needs some confidence in the child's ability to rely on the parent for comfort and on the child's readiness to co-create a large part of the child's autobiographical narrative.

How can the therapist know that a child is ready for this powerful intervention? One aspect is having seen the parent provide safety and comfort for the child. The caregiver should be able to tolerate the child's affect and not become dysregulated. Before beginning a role-play or psychodramatic re-enactment, I often ask a child, "If you could talk with your birth parent, what would you want to say to your birthparent and what questions would you like to ask?" If the child cannot discuss this in a session, that is clear evidence that the child is not ready to begin this powerful intervention. We might talk about this over several sessions and gradually, the child will often come up with very good questions and statements. The parent and the therapist may also make suggestions. Then I usually ask the child to write these statements and questions, or dictate it to the parent who can write it down, as if writing a letter to the birthparent. I make clear to the parent that it is not their job to make the child do this. As the child is ready, the child will write the letter. Once the child has been able to discuss this in a session and write the letter, then I am usually fairly confident that the child is ready to begin the psychodrama.

Developing the Reflective Function

There will be several major outcomes of this phase that fall under the umbrella of the reflective function. The reflective function (Fonagy et al., 2002) is the capacity to mentalize, to have a mental representation of self, other, and the relationship, and to think about these mental representations. For example, the reflective function is operating when a parent says, "I thought you were angry with me. I didn't know you were scared that I was angry with you." In order to state what the parent did, the parent had to have a mental representation of the child, the parent, and the relationship. The parent had one mental representation (that the child was angry) and then realized that this mental representation of the child and the relationship is not correct, that a different relationship is present.

The reflective function allows for the exploration of internal working models. By evoking and examining these internal working models, which operate largely outside of awareness, the therapist helps the client reconfigure these internal working models. The co-creation of new meanings is largely a reworking of an internal working model that developed in response to one set of relationships and experiences, but which now results in dysfunctional behavior because the relationships and experiences are now quite different.

Exploration leads to a more fully developed reflective function. The reflective function leads to greater insightfulness and also to less impulsivity and better affect regulation. The reflective function is also necessary for the co-creation of meaning and is at the heart of the affective/reflective dialogue. The reflective element of the affective/reflective dialogue is the operation of the reflective function, the ability to mentalize. In some regards the reflective function can be considered to be the hub of the wheel from which many of the other components of Dyadic Developmental Psychotherapy flow. Therapist use of self, a focus on process, intersubjectivity, affective/reflective dialogue, insightfulness, co-regulation of emotions, co-creation of meaning, follow-lead-follow, interactive repair, and the non-verbal/verbal dialogue all have the reflective function as an important dimension.

Summary

The Exploration phase of treatment has as its primary goal the examination of current and past relationships, events, experiences, and emotions, with the aim of achieving greater integration of these experiences into a coherent autobiographical narrative. One significant element of this examination is the exploration of how the past is affecting the present and how that may be the root of dysfunctional patterns. When current circumstances are markedly different that the circumstances in which internal working models developed, and when the parent or child has been deprived of the opportunity to revisit and reintegrate these internal working models, dysfunction can emerge. All behavior is adaptive. In many respects, dysfunctional behavior can be viewed as behavior that was adaptive, but because circumstances have changed, that behavior is no longer adaptive. Trauma activates the survival brain more than the learning brain; then opportunities for new learning of a healing nature are severely limited. The creation of a safe base for exploration allows for the exploration necessary to achieve integration and healing.

While all the components of Dyadic Developmental Psychotherapy are used in treatment, this phase focuses on the co-creation of meaning, the co-regulation of emotions, and the affective/reflective dialogue. PACE is a component that is ever present. Follow-lead-follow, the creation and maintenance of concordant intersubjective experiences, and the reflective function are also significant components of this phase.

The Exploration phase is a major phase in treatment. It requires physical, emotional, and psychological safety for the emergence and maintenance of a secure base. However, the therapist should not assume that this means that exploration cannot begin quite early in treatment. In fact, exploration can begin in the first session as an example earlier in this chapter illustrated. What exploration requires is the creation and maintenance of a secure base. As that secure base is strengthened exploration can deepen. There is not a bright white line between exploration and integration. Integration requires exploration, and as exploration occurs and goes deeper, integration becomes stronger.

INTEGRATION

Integration, the fourth phase, occurs on many levels during treatment. There is neurological integration, emotional integration, and psychological integration. Its hallmark is the capacity to see shades of gray instead of absolutes. Integration is seen when a child is able to hold disparate feelings at the same time. For example, integration is seen when the child is able to experience anger at a birthparent for not keeping the child safe or for abusing the child, while also being able to recall the times they enjoyed each other. Integration is an iterative process, and this process can begin quite early in treatment, even within the first session. The only precursors necessary for integration are the creation and maintenance of the secure base and associated alliance that provides the safety necessary for exploration to occur. Integration can be viewed as a developmental process in which themes, relationships, experiences, events, and one's narrative are reworked over time in a flexible manner. At important developmental stages this process is more easily achieved since this is a normal time for exploration and new integration to occur. For example, the brain is in a more flexible state and going through a period of reorganization and reintegration in early childhood and during adolescence. Treatment provides the structure and methods to facilitate this process and to help create the conditions necessary for successful integration.

One of the main symptoms of Post Traumatic Stress Disorder and Complex Trauma is dissociation, which can be viewed as a lack of integration. Dissociation and the associated trauma symptom of flashbacks represent a splitting off of explicit memory and episodic memory, which is largely a left hemisphere function, from implicit or emotional memory, which is largely a right hemisphere function. There is a profound difference between an integrated memory and a flashback. An integrated memory has both explicit or episodic elements and implicit or emotional elements. When recalling an integrated memory, one is recalling something that occurred in the past and knows that one is in the present remembering the past event. A flashback represents the dissociation of explicit from implicit memory. When a flashback occurs, the person is reliving and reexperiencing the emotions of the past in the present without the realization that one is recalling a past event. An example of explicit memory is when a parent comes up behind a child and places a hand on the child's shoulder, and the child says, "My foster father used to grab me there and pull me into the pantry for a spanking." In a flashback, the parent comes up behind a child, place a hand on the child's shoulder, and the child turns to hit the parent with a frightened and angry expression, while screaming, "Leave me alone, I didn't do anything." The child is reliving the experience. The experience of being touched on the shoulder evoked powerful emotions without the associated explicit or episodic elements. As a result, the child is experiencing strong emotions and then connects those emotions to whatever is occurring in the present that evoked those emotions, such as being touched by a parent, a look, or certain words.

For integration to occur, past events, situations, and experiences have to be reviewed and revisited (exploration) so that the internal working models can be made explicit, subject to exploration, and new meanings thereby created. It is the new meanings that represent a new integration of emotions and cognitions. It is most useful to think of integration as a process or spiral. In this view, developmental tasks run vertically, and integration is an ascending spiral that returns to each element in a deeper and deeper fashion. In this way the person achieves greater levels of integration over time.

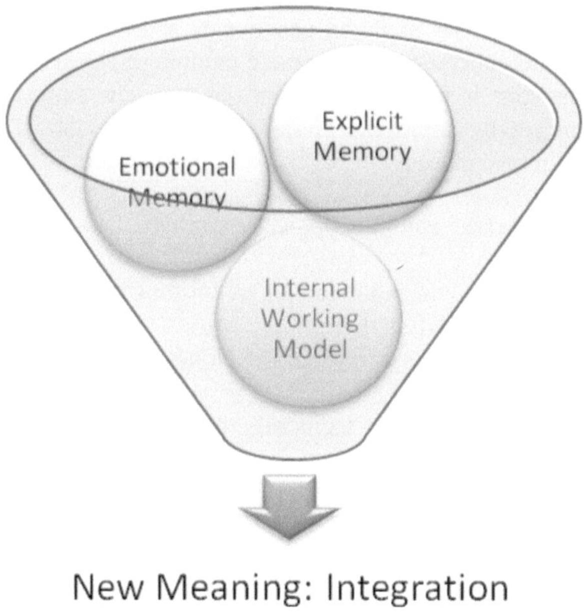

The primary task in this phase is the further development of a coherent autobiographical narrative that is not shame-based. Many people who have experienced complex trauma and disorders of attachment have an identity and narrative that is largely shame-based. These people often feel a deep sense of shame about themselves. The development of a coherent narrative that allows one to express personal potential is one outcome of the integration phase, healing. To achieve healing the therapist will focus on developing greater integration of elements of the past that have been dissociated and split off. The development of enhanced reflective abilities is a central component of this process.

While all of the components of Dyadic Developmental Psychotherapy will be used in the Integration phase, the primary components of treatment in this phase involve the affective/reflective dialogue and the co-creation of meaning. During this phase, the therapist may find that various methods to facilitate the cognitive processing of integration, for example from Cognitive Behavioral Therapy, can be useful. During this phase there is an emphasis on reviewing the client's life story, reflection on current status and past actions, and how these are related. As in the other phases, PACE remains a central component for the therapist of use.

Primary Tasks and Components

In this fourth phase the therapist has several primary tasks. The therapist's goal is to use the newly explored past events and internal working models to create a more coherent and integrated autobiographical narrative. In this phase the therapist is helping the client develop new and more functional and developmentally appropriate internal working models. The therapist's primary task in this phase is:

- Creating a coherent autobiographical narrative. This requires two additional elements:
  - Integration of trauma and reduction of splitting off
  - Enhanced reflective function
- The primary components of Dyadic Developmental Psychotherapy that are used in this phase are:
  - Co-creation of meaning, including the cognitive processing of new meanings
  - Affective/reflective dialogue
  - PACE

Other elements or processes that are important in this phase are:

- Review of life story and the journey taken
- Reflection on current status and past actions and how these may be related.

In many ways this phase and the previous one, Exploration, occur in tandem, in a cyclical fashion. Exploration of events leads to integration when there is an affective/reflective dialogue and activation of the reflective function. Integration then cycles back into exploration as the client's curiosity about the client's life draws the client into deeper exploration.

Creating a Coherent Autobiographical Narrative

Creating a coherent autobiographical narrative is a broad task. It includes the integration of split off memories and emotions, the development of an enhanced reflective function, greater capacity to tolerate strong emotions and to hold in mind conflicting emotions, and deeper self-knowledge.

Integration is the end product of exploration. The reflective element of the affective/reflective component is one of the components that can lead directly to greater integration. In the same way, at the end of each role-play or psychodramatic reenactment, time spent "debriefing" or talking and reflecting about the experience that just occurred will lead to greater integration of the experience. This ultimately creates healing. This ebb and flow of experience and reflection is the ebb and flow between the exploration phase and the integration phase. The steps involved in reading about events from the past in documents or engaging in a role-play, which evoke strong emotions in a titrated manner, and then reflecting on those past events and the emotions evoked, are what leads to integration of the experience and the co-creation of new meanings, which are one measure of healing.

At this point in the treatment process the therapist usually finds that the parents and child have a clearer sense that the therapist is there to help. This greater clarity regarding the therapist's intentions allows for the exploration and integration in a deeper way of more difficult situations and experiences. While the therapist may make mistakes of judgment or timing, these now tend to be viewed as honest errors because the family better understands the therapist's intentions. The repair of these mistakes by the therapist can usually proceed relatively quickly and smoothly.

The following example illustrates integration in treatment. Peter had a long history of being abused and neglected by his birth parents. He was removed from his birth family at the age of six because of multiple skull and arm fractures. Peter was in five foster homes, during the next three years. He was removed from one because of neglect and that foster home was closed. At age nine he moved into the Therapeutic Foster Home of Mr. and Mrs. Hunter and their three teenage sons. When Peter first moved into the Hunter home, he was still soiling himself, would hoard food in his bed, often took items not his without permission, and would become aggressive and violent toward Mrs. Hunter. Now eleven years old and after ten months of treatment, Mr. and Mrs. Hunter and Peter are reflecting on their recent interchange about Peter's difficulties in school with two bullies.

Mrs. Hunter: Peter came to me two weeks ago because two older girls were provoking him, saying mean things to him about him and us.
Therapist: Really? Peter, what was going on?
Peter: These two girls were being really mean. They'd say I was dumb and smelled bad. They'd say my mom was fat and all sorts of things that made me really mad.
Therapist: So what happened?
Peter: Well at first I just tried to handle it myself, and I didn't do so well. I'd get angry and start yelling, and I even pushed Eloise once, er twice, actually.
Therapist: So then you went to your parents?
Peter: Yes
Mr. Hunter: It was really good. We'd known something was going on because he'd gotten a few demerits in school for yelling at these two girls in the hall and pushing one.
Therapist: So, Peter, what made you go to your parents?
Peter: I realized what I was doing wasn't working. I also realized part of what made me so angry with those girls is that some of what they said and did reminded me of how my sisters would bully me and how my birthparents thought that was funny and would egg them on. I realized that I should tell Mom and Dad because they're not like my birth parents
Mrs. Hunter: When he told us what was going on, we realized that the school was only hearing one side of this. They'd see Peter yelling or pushing, but he didn't tell them what the girls had done to provoke him. After he told us, I called the principal and told her what was going on.
Peter: Yeah, she did, and I felt so good. Mom was helping me! (He says this in a happy loud voice with a big smile)
Therapist: You look so happy now about that.
Peter: You bet I am. Getting in trouble used to be what I was, but not now. Now, sometimes bad things happen, but I've got people to help me (looking from Mom to Dad with a big smile).
Mr. Hunter: What made me feel really proud of Peter was that he's been going to the guidance counselor every day to tell him what these girls are doing and saying. And guess what? Peter hasn't had any demerits in two weeks, and one of the girls was just suspended at the end of this week.
Therapist: Way to go Peter!

In this brief interchange we can see how the affective/reflective dialogue allows Peter and his parents to co-create a new meaning for Peter. The new meaning is that Peter can ask for help and receives it. This new meaning leads to a significant change in his self-concept, his feeling state, and his behavior.

Another illustration of an integrative experience is the following role-play with Rose and her foster/adoptive mother. In the previous section you read the transcript of a role play in which the therapist played Rose's birth mother, Sage, with Rose and her foster/adoptive mother. In that role play the therapist acted in a manner similar to the birth parent, and this allowed Rose to explore this experience from the past and rework it with a new and safer ending. In this new role play, Rose has the opportunity to achieve some closure and to integrate those past relationships into her current life so that she can move on with her life. Many adopted children and children in foster care feel a sense of divided loyalties. They often feel that they would have to let go of their birth family to be part of the new family, and this may feel like disloyalty to the child. This either/or view is a marker of a rigidity that exploration seeks to change. The reader can see a higher degree of integration here when Rose is able to "hear" and experience her birth mother's permission to both love her and love her new family. This both/and experience, the ability to hold seemingly conflicting emotions and thoughts in mind, is one of the hall marks of integration.

In many ways the "magic wand," which is what I call this second role-play, is an integrative and healing experience. In this role-play, instead of trying to act and speak like the character being portrayed, the actor presents the character as "healthy," or "normal," or "nice." The character will be communicating several important messages including:

- I am sorry for what I did.
- It is my "fault" not yours.
- I want you to be a part of this new family. It's ok to love them and let them love you.

Art: That's what you'd like to tell her? Hey, I have an idea! I have a good idea, I think. I can go have her come back, but this time, instead of being *mean* and trying to hurt you, this time I can make her come back and for just five minutes she can talk to you and be nice and talk to you in a nice way and then you could ask her questions if you wanted to ask her questions. What do you think about that? She won't be mean this time. I'll have her come back for just five minutes, and I can, with magic, (Rose hugs Jane) make her be a nice person for five minutes.
Jane: Do you want to ask her?
Rose: (whispers in Jane's ear) OK.
Art exits the room and then returns in blanket costume again as Sage. Seated on the couch, Jane holds Rose in her arms.
Sage: (in a friendly tone) Hello, Rose, I'm your first mommy, Mommy Sage, and I came back, I came back because I heard you wanted to ask me some things.

Jane: What do you want to ask her?
Rose: (in a small quiet voice) Why was you bad?
Sage: Why was I bad? Why was I mean?
Rose: (softly) Yeah.
Sage: Oh, you know (pause) I wasn't raised the right way. My mommy didn't raise me the right way, and I didn't know how to take care of a little baby or a little girl. I didn't know the right way to take care of you. And I didn't know how to take care of you and all the things you did that little babies do, I didn't know what to do so, and so I thought you were bad, but you weren't bad. I just didn't know how to take care of you. I wasn't very happy. I wasn't happy and I blamed you, but it wasn't your fault.
Rose: (In a small quite voice) It was your fault?
Sage: Yes, I wasn't very happy, and I couldn't think about all the things that were making me unhappy. So instead of thinking about what was making me unhappy, I blamed you (Rose watches Sage intently) but I shouldn't have done that (Rose pulls herself closer to Jane and Jane hugs her). I'm sorry I did that, Rose. (Rose curls up in Jane's arms.) I lost my temper with you sometimes. (Rose wriggles, watches Sage intently over her shoulder) I shouldn't have done that. I'm sorry that I, I'm sorry that I scared you when I hit you. Remember when I broke the TV?
Rose: (sitting very still, she nods her head)
Sage: Yeah. I'm sorry about that. I shouldn't have done that. *That* wasn't your fault.
Rose: (looks up into Jane's eyes, Jane nods and then Rose smiles.)
Jane: (to Rose) What else did you want to know?
Rose: (to Sage) Why you left?
Sage: Why I left?
Rose: Yeah?
Sage: 'Cause I just couldn't take care of you and I wasn't being a good mommy and I just wanted to do the things I wanted to do. I didn't know how to take care of a little girl. I didn't know what I was supposed to do. All I wanted to do was do the things I wanted to do and that's not what a mommy is supposed to. A mommy supposed to think about her children first. I didn't do that. I wasn't a very good mommy for you and I'm sorry about that. . . .
Rose: (Rose shifts her position a bit and takes hold of the collar of Jane's sweater.) You was. (Meaning that Sage was a good mommy)
Sage: I was?
Rose: Uh huh.
Sage: Well there's one thing, there's one I know I could do now that would be a good Mommy thing. You know what that is?
Rose: (playing with Jane's collar, while watching Sage intently) No.
Sage: The one thing I'd like to do now that I *think* would be a good mommy thing is I would like you to let Mommy, *this* mommy (pointing at Jane), Jane, I'd like you to let her be your mom. I think that would be a good thing. I think

the best thing I could do is say to you, “I want you to let her be your mommy” (Rose turns her gaze to Jane and looks into her eyes and smiles) and I want you to be her little girl.
Rose: (in a small quite voice) Thank you. (Rose sits up in Jane’s lap and hugs her, burying her face into Jane’s neck and hair. Jane tightens her arms around Rose.)
Sage: You’re welcome. Goodbye Rose.
Rose: Bye.
Sage: Bye-bye.
(Sage gets up, leaves the office and closes the door behind her.)
Jane: That makes you feel better?
Rose: Yes.
Jane: What part made you feel better?
Rose: She said sorry and that you can be my mommy now (giggles).
Jane: She said sorry and that made you feel better?
Rose: And that I can be your daughter.
Jane: She let you be my daughter and that made you feel better?
Rose: Yes.
Jane: Mmmm. So what do you think? So what do you think? Think we ought to move forward in this adoption?
Rose: Yes!
(Debriefing. Art returns to the room and sits down.)
Art: Who was that?
Rose: Mommy Sage.
Art: What did she tell you? What did she say? Tell me what happened!
Rose: (in a proud-sounding voice) I can be her daughter.
Art: Really?
Rose: Yeah.
Art: (looking at Rose and pointing to Jane) She says she wants you to be her daughter?
Rose: Yeah.
Art: Oh!
Jane: But tell him what she said that made the difference. What did she tell you? She was . . . ?
Rose. Thanks for putting on the magic spell on her.
Jane: But what did she tell you? She was what?
Rose: She was nice.
Jane: She was “what” for the mean things?
Rose: (leans back in Jane’s arms) Sorry.
Art: She was sorry for all those mean things she did?
Rose: Yeah.
Art: Ahhh. I’m so glad. I’m so glad she’s sorry about that.
Rose: (laughs and looks up at Jane and kisses her)
Art: And she wants you to be Mommy’s little girl?

Rose: (smiling) Yeah.
Art: That's nice.
Rose: (smiling broadly) Yeah
Art: Is that what you want?
Rose: I let her go away without me. I can be her daughter (looking at Jane and hugging her) and she can be my mommy!
Art: Mmhm. That's what you want to be? You want to be Mommy's little girl?
Rose: Yeah, she's so nice. (snuggling up in Jane's arms) Hold me. (to Art) Can you bring me a glass of hot chocolate?

Summary

The integration phase tends to occur in oscillation with the exploration phase. Exploration, when followed up with reflection and the affective/reflective dialogue, leads to integration, which is what creates healing. An important task of this phase is to co-create new meanings that reflect a reworking of old and often negative internal working models of the self, others, and relationships. The outcome of this phase is healing, which can be seen in a more coherent autobiographical narrative and in more varied, open, and flexible responses. What integration produces is time during which the learning brain is operating and less time during which the survival brain is functioning as if it were still back in the maltreating environment.

HEALING

This phase overlaps the other phases. Healing occurs throughout treatment. The development of an alliance is, in and of itself, healing. For many adults and children, the development of a safe and trusting alliance with positive affective dimensions is a source of solace and healing. The alliance can become a model for other relationships and help the client better understand self, others, and how to manage relationships. Maintaining and deepening the alliance is a healing experience for those with damaged capacities to experience intimacy. Exploration, which leads to integration, is healing, even in the absence of immediate integration. Once exploration is occurring, normal developmental processes will lead toward further integration, and integration is the essence of healing. In many respects, healing is a natural outgrowth of integration. Exploration requires reflection to become integrative. Said another way, when both emotional regulation and reflection are simultaneously occurring, integration is occurring. Integration is experienced as emotion and reflection co-occurring. Integration is a healing phenomenon.

The primary outcomes of healing are:

- The development of a more complex, nuanced, and integrated sense of self, a coherent autobiographical narrative.
- More well developed reflective function.

As treatment is ending, there is a more balanced and complex experience of self and others. Toward the end of treatment, the primary task to be accomplished is a review of and reflection on the treatment experiences. This review of the treatment experiences affords greater integration of the experience into the child's and family's narrative.

When healing is occurring and treatment will be ending, the primary intervention strategies include:

- Co-creation of new meanings
- Insightfulness and reflection
- Affective/reflective dialogue
- PACE

As treatment is drawing to a close, there is increased time spent reflecting on the treatment experiences and a celebration of how life is different. This is not to say that the therapist doesn't note and comment on positive experiences in each and every session. That is often an important element of each session; the reflection on what good has occurred. This reflection on positive changes and a celebration of the long and difficult journey is an important element of beginning to end treatment and integration of the experience. This process helps frame the treatment experience and find its place in the family narrative. During this process, all the components of Dyadic Developmental Psychotherapy will be evident.

The following example will illustrate this end of treatment reflection. In this example, Tina, who is eighteen, and her grandparents reflect on their experience of treatment. Seated on the couch are grandparents, Barbara and Joe. Granddaughter, Tina, is sitting between them. In the first part of this, Tina reflects on how the role-play deeply affected her. In the second part, the family reflects on how they are different.

Part I

Art: So, if you sort of reflect back, Tina, on how did . . . going back two, three, four years in your mind, how did you *see* your world at that point? How did you *see* your family? How did you *see* yourself? What was the lens through which you were filtering everything? How did you see everything back then?

Tina: I'm afraid that . . . I don't . . . I didn't really . . . I was very *selfish* back then, I think. I didn't really care about anyone . . .

Art: Oh.
Tina: . . . I was particularly angry. I don't know why. I was just like . . . *my* world was centered around *me* . . .
Art: Mhmm.
Tina: . . . and what was going to happen to me. I didn't care what happened to *nobody* else. I was worried about me, me, me. And now, I'm like, ask anybody, I'm like always trying to help and I'm very caring about others. I mean, I care about myself and take care of myself, but I'm also very outwardly. I help people, I'm very helpful and I care about others and what happens to them.
Barbara: Are you still as angry as you were?
Tina: (shakes her head and shifts attention from Art to Barbara) No! I'm very much more happier.
Barbara; (smiles and nods while looking at Tina)
Tina: And I mean, I actually, when you tell me things like that, that I really do feel a lot more happier and more calm and everything. (in a puzzled voice) I mean, I don't remember what I was angry about, but after we started seeing Dr. Becker-Weidman and after I started letting all my feelings out, I started to . . . that anger slowly, like evaporated, like water from a kettle, it just slowly went away.
Barbara: (nodding) Mmhmm.
Art: And you *had* things to be angry about . . .
Tina: (nods)
Art: . . . things that happened with your birth mom and all kinds of things to be angry about, and you know, a lot of it was sort of displaced. You had things you legitimately should have been angry about. It just, it got displaced onto your mom and your dad (Tina refers to her grandparents as Mom and Dad).
Barbara: I think one of the best, not even that, the *best* session, but one of the *good* sessions that we had was when your wife came in and pretended to be Tina's birth mother Erica . . .
Art: *Ah.* Uhuh.
Barbara: (turns to Tina) . . . and after that session is when we really kind of turned around. It was like you had permission from your mother to go ahead and love us and to not be, not wait for her, to get healed or whatever, to take you in and I thought that was the big turning point, too.
Art: I see. (to Tina) Do you remember that session?
Tina: (nods)
Barbara: (to Tina) Remember? We talked a lot about that session.
Art: (to Tina) So what was that one like for you?
Tina: It was very emotional.
Art: It *was*? So what do you remember about it? When it was all over, what was it that you came away with?
Tina: I didn't feel, I didn't feel, I started not to feel angry anymore, like "These people are my parents and I can love them. It's okay."
Art: . . . Wow! Doing that role-play, getting permission from Erika . . .

Tina: Yeah, that's it!
Art: . . . your birth mom in the role play that "Yes, be part of this family. These are your parents and I want you to be their child," freed you up.
Tina: (nodding in agreement and smiling). It really did a lot.

Part II

Art: Tina, How's the family different from your point of view? (Aside to Barbara and Joe) I'll ask you folks, too, in a minute.
Tina: Closer.
Art: And when you think back over the last couple years, the different things we talked about, the different sessions and whatnot, is there any one or any particular session that really stands out in your mind as being significant or a turning point for you in some way or another?
Tina: I think it was when I, when we talked about what happened (lowers voice), that time I went away.
Art: Um, which . . . ?
Tina: I'm talking about when, two years ago, oh, it was probably longer than that now, but when I got tooken out of the home.
Art: Oh, when you were thirteen . . . when you were thirteen, right?
Tina: (looks at Mom) I wasn't thirteen. I was more like ten.
Art: Ten?
Barbara: Ten? You came back at thirteen.
Tina: Yeah.
Art: Oh, that's right, okay, you came back at thirteen. That was when you said you made up that story about your granddad and got removed from the home by DSS.
Tina: Yeah, that's what I mean. I came back at thirteen.
Art: So it was *eight* years ago.
Tina: Yeah. I was able to get it all off my chest and talk about it with my mom and dad (looking at her grandparents).
Art: Okay
Tina: And I was just like, for all those years, I had just been thinking—"What are they *thinking* about?" "Do they *think* about that," "Do they *wonder*?"
Barbara: 'Cause nobody said anything when she came back. We just completely ignored it. We went on with our life together.
Art: Acted as if . . .
Barbara: . . . like nothing had ever happened.
Art: *Oh,* I understand now, I think. So you all never really sat down. So that was the first time you had sat down together to talk about what you had said, what you had done, and what happened. So that made a big difference! How did that make a big difference for you?
Tina: I kinda got it all off my chest, and I was able to see that no matter what happened, they'll always love me (wipes away tears).

Art: That was a big thing, huh? You really feel moved?
Tina: Yeah.
Barbara: (hands Tina some tissues)
Art: What are your tears about, sweetie?
Tina: Just that I, just that I, just that I kinda thought about that, and I kinda felt bad, and it's just still with me that (her voice is breaking with emotion) I never kinda realized how much they love me. They really love me no matter what.
Art: (leans over and takes her hand) Wow. You saw that they love you.
Tina: And I realize now that I'm important, they love me no matter what. I'm their child.
Barbara: (Passes a tissue to Joe then wipes her own eyes while he wipes his eyes.)
Art: You're really their daughter!
Tina: And I . . .
Barbara: (patting away tears) Oh, boy! (laughs)
Art: It doesn't matter what you do or what you say, you realized they love you no matter what. (Addressing the whole family) That must have been a hard time for all of you.
Barbara: It *was*.
Joe: Oh, *yeah*. (reflectively) Yup. (wiping his eyes again)
(The whole family is dabbing their eyes with tissues.)
Tina: (looking at Joe) I got Dad crying?!
(Barbara & Joe laugh.)
Tina: I'm thinking that, and I'm really happy that I'm loved like that. I'm *blessed*, you know?
Joe: It did away with the rotting elephant in the middle of the living room floor. The thing we all knew and never talked about.
Tina: (Nods in agreement, and wipes her eyes.)
Barbara: Exactly.
Art: Yeah, because it was something on everyone's mind that there was this thing, that you had said this thing, and I guess you'd never, you really hadn't had a chance, to say, "I'm sorry that I did that and I made the story up and I'm sorry." You were really afraid that if you brought it up again, then your mom and dad would be really mad at you.
Tina: (nods her head) That's right. I thought they'd be mad if I brought it up, that they were still mad about it.
Art: And I think you were surprised that they weren't mad at all, they didn't blame you . . .
Tina: (leans over to her mother and hugs her)
Barbara: (puts her arm around Tina)
Art: . . . and they just felt really bad for you. So, that was a real turning point for you and the family in this whole process.
Tina: (Nods and turns to Barbara. They look into each other's eyes, and Tina and Barbara smile with tears in their eyes.)

Art: (to Joe and Barbara) And what about the two of you? Any particular session or any particular things that happened that, as you reflect back, seemed like turning points for you?
Barbara: Oh, I think every time we came out here there was a little bit of progress. I could see it each time we came out here. Just knowing how to talk to her. Not really so much different from the way I talked to my other kids, but just phrasing things a little bit differently, and learning, learning how to do things a little bit differently. So I think we grew each week we came out here, (looking over at Joe) each visit we grew a little bit more . . . (Comment: Notice Barbara's use of the words, "my other kids," which reflects, I believe, a deep claiming of Tina as her child.)
Joe: I believe so, too. I believe that the big, the big thing that started to turn the ball around was basically the initial start when we turned around and (to Barbara) you changed your hours and then there was somebody with her all the time.
Art: Oh, that's right. You changed your hours so that Tina could be home with one of you and out of school.
Joe: Working that way and trying to reestablish the family, recreate, and then a milestone I would believe would be the "dead elephant in the middle of the living room floor" (he wipes his eyes). Because we felt that we knew what had happened, it wasn't that we didn't know. It was a case where we look at things, well, that's in the past (brushes the tears away), we go forward . . . (The "dead elephant" he is referring to is Tina's story that she'd made up about being hurt by Joe that led to her being removed from the home by social services. It took the family nearly two years of fighting to get Tina back home.)
Barbara: Just ignored it . . .
Joe: . . . you know, we didn't feel that it was something that should be discussed because it's over, we're not going to change it.
Art: I think I understand.
Joe: So why relive it, why dwell on it?
Art: So what happened?
Joe: And uh, but then the day that you brought it up and we talked about it on the way home and everything, I think that helped turn the corner a little more, you know? It was more of a rapid incline and then over the course of the two years or so, with everything else that came, we had progress all the time because we'd have events occur and then we'd discuss those events and you'd give us different direction on how we could handle it a little differently . . .
Barbara: (nods)
Joe: . . . and maybe handle it a little better and prevent the head-butting that was going on, and things just kept getting better. You know, so now we have methods, different communication procedures and methods that work . . .
Art: I see.
Joe: You know, tools that, we didn't have before to achieve the same ends. We've allowed Tina to grow and mature, because don't forget when we started,

we had a sixteen-year-old at one age and now we've got an eighteen-year-old who is eighteen. We've come a long way.
Art: You feel good about this.
Joe: When you talk to people, other people, that are more outside, looking in, and they have a more neutral view, and you talk to them and they have nothing but good praises about Tina . . .
Barbara: (nods in agreement)
Joe: . . . whereas before . . .
Art: Boy, that must be so nice to hear.
Barbara: It *is*. It is, because it used to be at work every time the phone rang, and I heard Sister Josephina's voice, I thought "Oh, my God, what are we in for now?!" and now . . .
Joe: Yeah, "what did Tina do this time?" because it was always Tina doing things . . .
Barbara: . . . and when she calls me now it's always the good things she's calling me for, so it's good. (pats Tina on her shoulder and smiles at her)
Art: What a difference!
Barbara: And she really doesn't call anymore, but she's called a couple of times. There's such a big difference.
Joe: When I see her at the school, when I see the guidance counselor, and talking to them, everybody praises Tina. I'm so proud of her.
Art: Wow, what a wonderful journey you've been on.
Joe: It is.
Barbara: I'm so proud of Tina. Thank you.

SUMMARY

This chapter described the five phases of Dyadic Developmental Psychotherapy:

- Creating an Alliance,
- Maintaining the Alliance or Secure Base
- Exploration
- Integration
- Healing

These phases are grounded in Attachment Theory and based on secure attachment processes. The therapist acts as a guide helping the family navigate these phases with PACE as a primary framework. As previously mentioned, these phases are presented in a discrete manner for pedagogic purposes here. In practice, the phases overlap and as the therapist and family move through treatment, and circle back and forth among the states even within one session. However, the basic framework is that healing is grounded in integration,

integration comes from exploration, exploration requires a secure base, and the secure base develops from an emotionally meaningful and positive alliance.

It all begins with creating an alliance. The alliance is the root from which treatment grows. The primary task of this beginning is to create a secure base for exploration, integration, and healing. The therapist's primary tasks in this phase include the following:

- Forming a therapeutic alliance with the caregivers and the child.
- Developing a treatment contract, a shared mutual understanding of the work together.
- Forming initial theories of behavior and meanings to be explored.
- Ending with the initial creation of a secure base.

In this phase the primary intervention components of Dyadic Developmental Psychotherapy are the following:

- Creating concordant intersubjective experiences
- Follow-lead-follow with an emphasis initially on follow
- PACE, which is an important component throughout treatment
- Co-regulation of emotions
- Therapist use of self
- A focus on connections and not compliance.

The Maintaining the Alliance phase begins with the creation of a secure base, which is an outcome of the previous phase. The alliance is fragile and must be maintained carefully. Children and adults who have experienced chronic maltreatment within a caregiving relationship are wary of intimacy and fearful of trusting others. The therapist must put effort into maintaining this newly developing alliance; it must be carefully nurtured. In this phase the therapist's goal is to develop and expand the secure base for exploration, integration, and healing. The primary tasks in this phase include the following

- Deepening and strengthening the therapeutic alliance,
- Managing emotional closeness and distance,
- Exploring initial theories of behavior and the meanings to be explored,
- Interactive repair. Paying particular attention to repairing relationship breaches.

The components of Dyadic Developmental Psychotherapy that are used in this phase are PACE, intersubjectivity, follow-lead-follow, and interactive repair.

While many people may consider the Exploration Phase to be the sine-quo-non of treatment, it would be a serious mistake to discount the importance of creating and maintaining the alliance. Without an alliance there can be no secure base, and without a secure base there can be no exploration. Exploration can begin as soon as there is some degree of psychological, emotional, and physical safety and this can occur within the first session. There is always some exploration, even in "pre-treatment" evaluation sessions. In families with caregivers who have significant unresolved trauma, the therapist must exercise caution. If exploring the child's trauma will be dysregulating for the adult or if it triggers the caregiver's unresolved trauma in a way that leads to shaming or blaming by the caregiver, then deeper work with the child will require that the parent's unresolved issues be addressed. Exploration requires safety.

In the Exploration Phase the therapist has several primary tasks. The therapist's goal is to explore history, memories, events, and experiences that continue to shape relationships and that continue to affect behavior and functioning. The objectives of this phase include exploring how the past is alive in the present, exploring internal working models, exploring initially the meanings of events and behavior, and developing the reflective function. The primary components of Dyadic Developmental Psychotherapy that are used to pursue these objectives include the co-creation of meaning, the co-regulation of affect, PACE, intersubjectivity, follow-lead-follow, the affective/reflective dialogue, interactive repair, the reflective function, and insightfulness.

Integration is a direct result of exploration and may be thought of as occurring in tandem with exploration. The exploration of internal working models, relationships, and past events as active in the present in a reflective manner leads to greater integration. The behavioral effects of integration can be seen in greater impulse control, better affect regulation, and a more nuanced view of self, others, and relationships. During the Integration Phase, there is greater coherence of the person's autobiographical narrative. The therapist facilitates the development of new and more functional and developmentally appropriate internal working models, which are essential for the creation of a more coherent and integrated autobiographical narrative. In order to create this more coherent autobiographical narrative, the reflective function and insightfulness must be developed. These goals can be achieved through the use of PACE, affective/reflective dialogue, and the co-creation of new meanings.

The objective of treatment is healing. Healing occurs throughout treatment. As treatment approaches an ending, the Healing phase predominates. The primary marker of this phase is the development of a more complex, integrated, and nuanced autobiographical narrative. The client will have a more well-developed reflective function and be able to regulate affect arousal

Table 5.1. Phases and Components

	PHASE				
COMPONENT	DEVELOPING ALLIANCE	MAINTAINING ALLIANCE	EXPLORATION	INTEGRATION	HEALING
THERAPIST USE OF SELF	3	3	2	1	3*
CONNECTIONS NOT COMPLIANCE	3	3	2	1	1
PACE	3*	3*	3*	3*	3
INTER-SUBJECTIVITY	3*	3*	3*	2	1
REFLECTIVE FUNCTION	1	2	3	3*	3*
AFFECTIVE/ REFLECTIVE DIALOGUE	3	3	3*	3*	3*
COMMITMENT	3	3	3	3	3
INSIGHTFULNESS	1	1	3*	3	3*
COHERENT NARRATIVE	1	1	2	3*	3*
CO-REGULATION OF AFFECT	3*	3	3*	1	1
CO-CREATION OF MEANING	2	3	3*	3*	3*
FOLLOW-LEAD-FOLLOW	3*	3*	3*	2	1
INTERACTIVE REPAIR	3*	3*	3*	2	1
NON-VERBAL/ VERBAL DIALOGUE	3	3	3	2	1

While each component has a place in every phase of treatment and in every session, the relative importance or emphasis varies phase by phase and even session by session, depending on the family dynamics and the dynamics of the particular session; that is the art of treatment. For exposition purposes, the components are weighted on a scale of 1 (somewhat important), 2 (important), 3 (very important). Within each phase, the components are highlighted as being particularly important and are marked with an asterisk (*). It is not that the other components are unimportant; it is that these three tend to be more significant for moving into and through that particular phase. The reader will see, for example, that PACE is a very important in all phases of treatment. And certainly the therapist's use of self is important throughout treatment, although how the therapist uses self varies by phase.

more independently and effectively. During this phase the therapist will find that there is more reflection about the treatment experience and the changes that have occurred. The child will be able to, without shame, reflect on past negative experiences in a thoughtful and regulated manner. During this phase several components of Dyadic Developmental Psychotherapy predominate. The co-creation of new meaning, insightfulness and reflection, affective/reflective dialogue, and PACE are all central to this phase.

Table 5.1 summarizes this chapter's discussion of phases and the differential use of the various components of Dyadic Developmental Psychotherapy in each phase. It is presented as a guide for thinking about practice and is not meant to be prescriptive.

Chapter 6

Primacy of Parents

In this chapter I describe the importance of parenting and parents to the practice of Dyadic Developmental Psychotherapy. While Dyadic Developmental Psychotherapy is a broad approach to treatment and can be used with individuals and couples, it is a family therapy approach that focuses on relationship as a primary means of effecting change. When working with children who have experienced complex trauma, disorders of attachment, and significant maltreatment, the therapeutic involvement of the caregivers (birth, adoptive, foster parents, or other caregivers) is central to treatment outcome. In this book I use the term "parent" and "parents" broadly to include all types of primary caregivers, including residential care staff and foster parents.

WHY ARE PARENTS NECESSARY FOR TREATMENT SUCCESS?

Trauma and attachment difficulties are primarily relational in nature. Children generally live in families and rely on primary caregivers. Dyadic Developmental Psychotherapy is primarily a relationship-based treatment. So, primary caregivers, parents, play a primary role in treatment. The best predictor of treatment outcome is not the answer to the question, "How disturbed is this child?" The best predictor of treatment outcome is the parent's capacity to implement attachment facilitating parenting. The best predictor of treatment outcome is the parent's state of mind with respect to attachment, commitment, insightfulness, reflective function, sensitivity, and the capacity to create and engage in positive concordant intersubjective experiences with the parent's child. Parents are the keystone of treatment success. As a general rule, whatever the therapist is hoping the parents will do in relationship with their child, the therapist must do with the parent. A danger that sometimes snares therapists is becoming aligned with the child against the parent; "If only these parents would see what a great kid they have, everything would be ok." Parents of children with trauma and attachment disorders require empathy, support, and understanding. Once the therapist recognizes how critical it is that parents be "on board," then focusing on the parents becomes second nature.

Children live with their primary caregivers. Most of their waking hours are spent with these people, so the parents and the home they create will have a profound impact on their child. These statements are not meant to blame parents or hold them responsible for the difficulties they face. They may not have created the damage that their children brought into their home, but they do have the responsibility to help heal their child's wounds. Parents have a tremendous impact on the lives of their children.

As previously described, healing requires integration, which develops as a result of exploration, which requires a secure base, which is built on an alliance. The therapist begins by building an alliance with the parents. This is essential for creating a secure base for exploration. With some families, this may only take part of one meeting with the parents. For other caregivers it may take many meetings. By focusing on the important tasks at each phase the therapist can determine what work needs to be done and how far along are the family and therapist. For some families, building the alliance may begin by providing case management services and securing various entitlements for the family. While "case-management" and helping parents secure food-stamps, subsidized housing, or an IEP for their child may not be defined as "psychotherapy," it is therapeutic in that it facilitates the primary task of creating an alliance. It is a means for the therapist to demonstrate concretely that the therapist understands the family and can be of value to the family.

Therapeutic endeavors should be consistent with the principles, components, and underlying theory of the approach. For this reason, during the assessment, the first meeting is with the parents, and when treatment begins, the first sessions are with the parents. Primary caregivers are central to treatment success. The methodology of practice should be consistent with this underlying principle. Therefore, the therapist starts by building an alliance with the parents. The therapist meets with the primary caregivers to underscore their central role in the treatment process. The therapist continues meeting with the caregivers until the therapist feels comfortable that the caregivers have enough of an understanding of the principles and approach of Dyadic Developmental Psychotherapy to facilitate therapeutic work. When the therapist discovers with the family that the caregiver's past histories have unresolved elements that interfere with the parents being the parents they'd like to be, then the therapist needs to explore these issues. All of the components, principles, and methods previously described would be used by the therapist to help the parents resolve these unresolved elements from their past. It is a serious error to attempt to begin treatment with the child, either individually or in a family context, if the parents' unresolved issues interfere with their current capacity to create and provide the safety necessary for treatment.

Assessing Parent Capacity

Assessing parent capacity to provide safety, and the capacity to be reflective, insightful, sensitive, and to have a reasonably strong commitment to this child are important components of treatment. These caregiver capacities can be assessed either informally or using more formal methods (Becker-Weidman, 2010). In either case it is essential for the therapist to have some measure of the caregiver functioning along each of these dimensions so that the pace of treatment is consistent with the parent's capacities and abilities. Having a measure of the caregiver's functioning along each of these dimensions also provides the therapist with a potential set of directions regarding treatment. Can the therapist begin right away with the family? Does the therapist need to do some work with the parents? Can the therapist work along concurrent paths and work with the family and child and also with the parents separately? How best to effect this? These are all questions the therapist will need to consider as treatment begins. This next section will briefly outline some formal methodologies that the therapist can use to assess caregiver capacities.

Informal Questions During the Interview

While the formal methodologies below can be quite helpful for therapists who wish to use a more standardized approach, using one's clinical judgment can also produce very useful and important insights. A few of these less formal approaches will be described in this section.

Patterns of Attachment

Patterns of attachment can be gleaned from how the client responds to emotionally evocative questions that probe the client's relationship with significant others and caregivers. Broadly speaking, the major patterns of attachment may be characterized by the types of responses in table 6.1. These patterns are not diagnoses and the descriptions provided are meant to be only a suggestion or guide. Based on the therapist's training and experience, the clinician can use this characterization as a guide to anticipate how the caregiver may manage emotionally evocative experiences in treatment. With this

Table 6.1. Characteristic Responses of the Four Main Patterns of Attachment

Pattern of Attachment	*Characteristic Responses*
Secure	Coherent, collaborative, concise, and consistent dialogue. There is a clear valuing of relationships and emotions with objectivity. Descriptions and evaluations of attachment related experiences are consistent, whether the experiences were positive or negative. Responses are complete and concise; providing enough detail to fully answer the question without bringing in unnecessary tangential or irrelevant material.
Avoidant	Responses are consistently sparse with little if any supporting details. The responses are dismissing of emotional content. Over use of "normalizing" and generalized representation of history without any supporting details. Over use of such descriptors as "normal," "excellent," "typical," "usual." Responses are overly brief and without sufficient detail to convincingly answer the question.
Preoccupied	Responses are consistently overly long and rambling with a large amount if irrelevant detail. The person is preoccupied with or by past relationships and experiences. The client often appears angry, passive, or fearful. Sentences are often long, grammatically tangled and filled with vague usages. There is a large amount of irrelevant material brought into the dialogue.
Disorganized	Responses are often unorganized showing a marked lapse in the monitoring of reasoning and of the discourse. As an example, the person may describe a deceased person in the present tense as if still living. There may be prolonged silences during the dialogue or speech that may be characterized as eulogistic.

guide in mind, the therapist can focus on the caregiver's strengths and use the components of treatment most likely to be most helpful.

Insightfulness & Reflective Function

When discussing the child, it can be quite revealing to ask the parents what they think makes the child act in a particular way. The manner in which they respond to this question can reveal a lot about their insightfulness and their reflective abilities. When meeting with a couple, I find it very useful to ask each member of the couple, "Of all the things your child does, what most gets under your skin, or gets you annoyed or irritated? What do you find most difficult to deal with?" Most often I find that each member of the couple will describe something different. I then will ask, "What is it about XXX (what one parent identified) that makes that more (whatever word they use: frustrating, annoying, irritating, etc.), than YYY (what the other identified)." Or, I might ask, "Why do you think it is that you find XXX so disturbing?" The therapist does not necessarily need to find deep or revealing insights.

However, it is helpful to know why the parents feel the way they do and what that might mean in terms of the parents' past history or experiences.

Mrs. Kane brought her twins in for treatment. As we discussed the twins, the following interchange occurred:

> Therapist: Now, that's really interesting. You find Sharon's passive non-compliance much more irritating that Shawn's throwing and breaking things. I wonder why that is?
> Mrs. Kane: (laughs while saying) Well, when you put it that way, it does seem strange. He sure has destroyed some things around the house.
> T: So, why do you think that is?
> K: I don't know. I guess manners were always really important to my Momma. I also find it easier to cope with the Shawn's being so direct with his anger, but Sharon's sneaky ways, I just don't know what to do with her.
> T: Oh, so part of it is that, maybe, you feel secure in how to handle Shawn, but with Sharon you don't feel as certain?
> K: Yes, that makes sense. I'm at a loss with Sharon and that makes me feel like I don't know what I'm doing. I guess that's it. I don't like not knowing what to do.

Commitment

The best predictor of placement stability is a parent's commitment (Dozier & Lindheim, 2006). So, assessing the caregiver's commitment to this child can be a very important factor in how treatment may progress and in how the therapist may proceed. How can the therapist informally assess a caregiver's level of commitment? Certainly when a caregiver begins discussing disrupting the placement, there may be an obvious lack of commitment. This issue must be resolved before family treatment with the child can begin. There may be understandable reasons for the erosion in commitment that occurred over time. When there are signs of a decreased or low level of commitment by the parent for the particular child being discussed, the therapist should avoid trying to convince the parent to feel differently. While disruption is very painful and disturbing for everyone involved, trying to convince the parent to reconsider will primarily serve to turn what should be an intra-personal conflict into an inter-personal conflict between therapist and parent. In these instances what is often most helpful is ACE. Accept what the parent is describing, be curious about this to go deeper in an emotionally meaningful way, and provide lots of empathy. Helping the parent reflect on how the parent felt immediately before the placement, remembering the parent's hopes and dreams, can be very helpful. Exploring how those feeling changed over time may allow a parent to reach a decision that will be best for all involved. The questions about commitment in the previous chapter on the main elements of Dyadic Developmental Psychotherapy can be used to assess commitment.

Formal Methodologies

There are a number of more formal methodologies that can be used to assess state of mind with respect to attachment, insightfulness and reflective function, and commitment. In this section I will very briefly describe these approaches. The interested clinician is encouraged to study these topics in more detail by reading the references cited and by receiving additional training where indicated.

State of Mind with Respect to Attachment

The most researched, reliable, and valid tool to assess a person's state of mind with respect to attachment is the Adult Attachment Interview (Hesse, E., 2009). The interview protocol consists of twenty questions with various probes (Main, M., 1996). The use of this instrument for research purposes requires extensive training and validation. More recently there has been recognition that the instrument has significant value as a clinical tool for use in clinical practice (Steele & Steele, 2008). Using the questions and then applying one's clinical judgment can yield very useful information. A more formal methodology for interpreting the results can be found in Crowell & Owens (1998). When interpreting the client's responses, it is primarily the manner in which the questions are answered rather than the content that is used to determine the person's state of mind with respect to attachment. In other words, the therapist if focused on how the client responds to the questions.

Broadly speaking, the responses to the Adult Attachment Interview (AAI) questions are evaluated on two dimensions. One dimension is coherence, which refers to responses that provide a clear and convincing description, are truthful, succinct, and complete, and are presented in a clear and orderly manner. The four elements of coherence are quality, quantity, relevance, and manner. Quality refers to responses that are truthful and supported by clear and convincing evidence. An example of a response that is deficient in quality would be:

> Therapist: You described your childhood relationship with your mother as "loving." Can you think of a memory or an incident that would illustrate why you chose to describe the relationship as "loving?"
> John: Yes, she was caring and generous with me.

The next example illustrates a response that shows the elements of quality.

> Therapist: You described your childhood relationship with your mother as caring and generous. Can you think of a memory or incident that would illustrate why you chose to describe the relationship as caring and generous?
> Paul: Yes, she was caring and generous. I remember on my sixth birthday we didn't have much money that year, Dad had been laid off. I had just learned how to ride a two-wheeler and wanted my own bike. Mom somehow found the

money to buy me a second-hand bike and Dad fixed it up for me. That birthday present was such a surprise. I know that Mom used the money she'd been saving for a new dress for herself to buy that bike.

Quantity refers to responses that are succinct and complete. The answers are as informative as is necessary to fully respond but no more so than that. Relevance refers to responses that are relevant, that directly address the intent of the question and that do not include tangentially or superficially related material. Manner refers to responses that are clear and orderly and that avoid obscurity of expression, or ambiguity. The response should be a brief, complete, and orderly.

The second dimension is the person's ability to reflect on the motives of others. Examples of this sort of question from the AAI include the following: "Now I wonder if you could tell me, to which parent did you feel the closest, and why? Why isn't there this feeling with the other parent?" (Main, 1996, p. 6), or "Why do you think your parents behaved as they did during your childhood?" (Main, 1996, p. 8).

Insightfulness and Reflective Function

The formal methodology for the Insightfulness Assessment (Koren-Karie et al., 2002; Oppenheim and Koren-Karie, 2002) involves video-taping four episodes between the parent and child. These four episodes are about ten to fifteen minutes in length. The four episodes can be first free play in the play room, then a teaching task, a competitive game, and a nurturing activity. The therapist then selects a two-minute segment from each segment and shows each segment to the parent followed by a set of questions. The questions are:

What do you think went through <name of child>'s mind? What did <name of child> feel and think during this segment?

Is this segment characteristic of <name of child> more generally? Does it tell you something about <name of child>'s personality or characteristics?

I would now like to ask you about what you felt, while watching this segment. Did anything concern you, surprise you, or make you happy in this segment?

After all segments are viewed, then the following general questions can be asked:

First, from what we talked about during this interview until now, and from what you know about <name of child> in general, what characterizes <name of child> as a person, as a child? What makes <name of child> <name of child>? I will write down what you say and ask you for examples later on.

Based on how well you know your child, are there things about <name of child> that surprise you, concern you, or make you happy?
What is the thing that, in your opinion, most characterizes the relationship between your child and yourself?

The therapist can use clinical judgment and experience to evaluate the responses provided by the parent. This clinical use of the Insightfulness Assessment relies on the therapist's professional experience and training. Dyadic Developmental Psychotherapy provides the therapist with an attachment-theory framework and a family-focused relationship based perspective that is very informative in evaluating the responses to the above questions.

Commitment

As described above and in a previous chapter, the Commitment Assessment (Dozier & Lindheim, 2006) is a formal methodology to assess a caregiver's commitment to a specific child. There are several questions that are asked of the parent about the child. Some of these questions, from Dozier & Lindheim, 2006 p. 344, are:

1. (For foster placements) Do you ever wish you could raise (child's name)?
2. How much would you miss (child's name) if your child had to leave?
3. How do you think your relationship with (child's name) is affecting (child's name) right now?
4. How do you think your relationship with (child's name) will affect your child in the long-term?
5. What do you want for (child's name) right now?
6. What do you want for (child's name) in the future?

The clinician can use clinical judgment and experience to interpret and infer from the responses the caregiver's level of commitment.

A high level of commitment is characterized by the caregiver providing evidence of a strong emotional investment in and bond with the child and in parenting the child. Descriptions of the child and the parent-child relationship clearly reflect a strong connection with the child. The child is fully integrated into the family and all family activities.

An intermediate level of commitment is characterized by the caregiver providing evidence of investment in the child, but this is not clearly as deep as a parent scoring high on commitment. There may be some indices of high levels of commitment. There also is evidence suggesting that the child has not been psychologically adopted by the caregiver. For example, the parent may state that the parent would miss the child if the child left the family, but this is more of a matter-of-fact statement and lacks the strong emotional component seen in parents with a high level of commitment. The caregiver may describe limiting the psychological bond with the child but will also give evidence of struggling with this issue. The child may only be only partially integrated into the family. For example, the child is placed in respite care when the family goes on vacation. Overall, the therapist may conclude that the child is adequately cared for and nurtured but not to any special degree.

A low level of commitment is characterized by the caregiver providing virtually no evidence of a strong and active emotional investment in the child or in parenting the child. The caregiver may be indifferent to whether the child remains in the parent's care or may actually state that the parent hopes/desires the child will be removed. There is little evidence that the caregiver would miss the child.

SUMMARY

This chapter described the importance of parents and primary-caregivers for successful treatment. Parents are the keystone of treatment outcomes. Caregiver capacities to be reflective, insightful, sensitive, responsive, and committed are essential elements for positive treatment outcomes. The primary caregiver's pattern of attachment or state of mind with respect to attachment is a pivotal element. Caregivers with secure patterns of attachment are much more likely to be able to create and provide the healing PLACE that children with complex trauma and disorders of attachment require. There is ample evidence that the best predictor of a child's state of mind with respect to attachment is that of the primary caregivers (Cassidy & Shaver, 2008). Research has demonstrated that the best predictor of placement stability is caregiver commitment (Dozier & Lindheim, 2006). So it is very important for the therapist to assess these elements. Assessment can be done either using formal or informal methodologies. Treatment with families whose parents have unresolved issues that interfere with any of these dimensions of parent capacity will require more time and a slower pace of treatment. The therapist cannot neglect to create a healing therapeutic setting for the primary caregivers so that they are able to create a healing place for their child.

When the caregivers are found to have significant unresolved trauma in their history that interferes with their capacity to be sensitive, responsive, insightful, committed, and reflective, then the therapist will have to work more closely with them. In these instances the therapist may work with the parents for quite some time before involving the child. If the family lacks commitment and seems to want to disrupt the placement, the therapist has an obligation to continue to support the caregivers and explore various options that, under the circumstances, will be best for the child and caregivers. The next chapter discusses these situations in more detail.

Building an alliance with the primary caregivers is the first order of business in beginning treatment. The stronger is that alliance, the further along and the faster treatment may be able to proceed. A general principle is that whatever the therapist would like the parents to be able to do with the child, the therapist will need to be able to do with the parents. Providing a treatment setting for the primary caregiver that is sensitive, reflective, insightful, and rich with empathy will allow a secure base to develop with sufficient depth and security to allow exploration, integration, and healing. This setting will then transfer to the home environment for the child.

Chapter 7

Parents Are the Keystone

If parents are the keystone of treatment, then the proper preparation of caregivers to engage in treatment and create a healing PLACE is a necessary and essential component of the treatment process. This chapter provides an overview of this necessary and essential component. The approach being described is an approach to parenting and parent training grounded in the components and principles of Dyadic Developmental Psychotherapy. A much more detailed account of parenting and parent training consistent with Dyadic Developmental Psychotherapy can be found in the book *Attachment Parenting* (Becker-Weidman & Shell, 2010) and in several other publications (Becker-Weidman et al., 2005/2008; Becker-Weidman, 2006; Hughes, 2007; Hughes, 2009; Ring 2005/2008). For that reason, this will be a brief chapter and the interested reader is directed to the book *Attachment Parenting*, edited by Arthur Becker-Weidman and Deborah Shell (2010) for more details and specific recommendations and suggestions.

Working with caregivers begins with the first contact on the telephone, the manner in which the therapist listens to the caller, and arranges that first meeting. If the therapist begins with an assessment, which is strongly recommended, arranging for the first meeting to be with caregivers without the child sends a powerful message that is consistent with the principle that caregivers are the keystone of treatment. It is a good idea to start with a thorough assessment of the family, parents, and child so that important dynamics, such as sensory-integration issues, alcohol-related neurological dysfunction, or cognitive impairments are not overlooked or misconstrued (Becker-Weidman, 2007; Becker-Weidman, 2010).

Parent "education" is one component of building a working relationship with the caregivers. The same components of Dyadic Developmental

Psychotherapy and the processes or phases previously discussed apply to this work. During the assessment the therapist has the opportunity to begin building an alliance with the caregivers. Listening to the caregivers, guided by PACE, will help create the alliance necessary to create the secure base with the caregivers. Helping parents learn about and then effectively use attachment-facilitating parenting principles and methods is the therapist's objective at this point. How the therapist does this can enhance the alliance or damage it. It is vital that the therapist begins where the caregivers are and uses PACE to engender their engagement.

CHANGING THE LENS

Helping caregivers see below the surface behavior and catch a glimpse of the underlying emotions and perceptions driving that behavior is the first step in helping parents change the lens through which they view their child. The parent's assumptions and understandings about the child's motives, intentions, and purpose directly determine how the parent sees the person and experience, and this directly affects how the parent feels about the child and the experience. For example, a child is found in her room with her brother's juice box and other food items in the closet, behind some boxes. If the parent's understanding of this situation is that the child stole the items and was hiding, and being sneaky, the parent will feel one way toward the child, probably annoyed and frustrated. If this has been the umpteenth time the parent told the child not to steal her brother's juice boxes and hide food in her closet, and each time the child agrees with the parent not to do that, the parent may now be feeling quite upset with the child. On the other hand, if the parent understands the child's behavior as being driven by a different set of motives and intentions, the parent will feel quite differently. For example, if the parent goes deeper and sees that the child has grown up in settings in which there was inconsistent caregiving, a lack of any reliable source of food, and no one to help the child, then the parent may view the child's behavior as reflecting that experience and being driven by fear of going hungry and a belief that the only one she can count on is herself. In this instance, the parent may have much more empathy for the girl and respond accordingly. By helping parents see below the surface and understand the forces driving behaviors, the therapist can help parents feel differently and then act differently toward their child.

"All behavior is adaptive" and "kind attributions" are two important principles for the therapist to communicate to the parents. All behavior is adaptive refers to the notion that one develops in response to people, situations, relationships, and experiences that shape how a person feels and acts. Behaviors develop that are adaptive to the situation in which those behaviors originally formed. In many respects "symptoms" can be viewed as behaviors that were adaptive and that evolved in response to a specific set of circumstances, but these same symptoms now occur in new situations in which the behaviors are no longer adaptive. The new situations are inhibited from having an effect on these old behaviors if the old experiences evoked the stress response system on a chronic basis. In these instances it is the survival brain and not the learning brain that is primarily active. The survival brain does not function to incorporate new information, experiences, or emotions. This is one of the reasons it is so important for parents to understand this, so that they can focus on creating a healing PLACE at home with a deep sense of safety: emotional, psychological, and physical.

Recognizing that all behavior is adaptive as a principle can help parents look below the surface when presented with difficult behaviors by their child. Rather than trying to "manage" or stop behavior, it is much more effective to discover what is the driver or motivation for the behavior and address that underlying engine. This can be difficult for parents to do when they are in the middle of some experience with their child at home, at the mall, in the grocery store, or at church. By helping parents focus on this principle, *all behavior is adaptive*, the parents will be encouraged to consider thinking about "what is going on here?" or "I wonder what is making my child act this way?" The responses to these questions can lead the parent deeper and into more effective experiences which create security for their child.

An example may serve to illustrate the previous point. Six-year-old Tanya and her father, Jared, are at the grocery store. Jared has just told Tanya that they would not be getting Cocoa Puffs® but would get another cereal (Tanya is allergic to chocolate). A few moments later "suddenly" Tanya starts to yell loudly, "NO! You can't make me!" as she starts flailing in the shopping cart. Jared's first thought is to tell her, "Stop yelling, you can't have Cocoa Puffs® and that's it!" He's feeling exposed and embarrassed by his daughter's tantrum. But then he wonders, "Is something else going on?" At that moment he notices the tall bald man walking down the aisle and recalls that Tanya's birth father shaved his head and that there was a lot of very violent domestic violence in Tanya's birth home. So, Jared, thinking that Tanya may be scared, picks her up out of the shopping cart, hugs her and whispers into her ear, "You are safe, Honey. I'm here, and I'll keep you safe, OK, Honeybun?" Tanya blinks like she is waking up and looks at him, stops squirming, and says, "OK, Daddy." Was Jared right about what he assumed was causing Tanya's episode? Maybe and maybe not. What did happen is that Jared took a moment to consider what might be making his daughter so upset (scared?).

He then responded in a calming manner. That is the essential element. Jared created a bubble of safety, comfort, and security that calmed his daughter. He did for her what she was unable to do for herself, regulate her upset. This raises another important point for parent training within the context of Dyadic Developmental Psychotherapy. Parents set the rhythm, tone, and emotional climate for the family and for the child. Jared acted in a way that was responsive to Tanya and engaged her a manner that led to her responding to him and his emotional state rather than Jared amplifying Tanya's emotional upset by becoming emotionally upset.

The principle of *kind attributions* is related to the principle of *all behavior is adaptive and has meaning*. This principle is that when in doubt, attribute benign motivations or intentions to the child. Helping a parent have kind attributions regarding their child's intentions is more likely to lead to the creation of positive concordant intersubjective experiences and the creation of safety and security, which is most conducive to the functioning of the learning brain. The following example illustrates this point. Roger and Kathy adopted Keli from Columbia when she was four years old. During our first interview they described how now, by age nine, "She is still stealing food and hoarding it in her bedroom. Whatever she wants, she just steals, at home, in school, at the store." They described how when they'd catch her, she'd first "lie" about stealing, then have a tantrum, and much later say she was sorry, but her behavior never changed. Roger and Kathy had gotten to the point where they felt their home as like a jail, with food locked up and their having to search Keli's backpack every day before and after school. In our first meeting, which was just with Roger and Kathy, we discussed Keli's background, what they imagined and knew it was like for her, and how that might still, possibly, be affecting her. Afterwards, the following dialogue occurred.

Roger: She was hungry all the time in the foster home in Columbia. When we got her, Keli was so thin she was underweight. She put on ten pounds right after we got her.
Kathy: So food's always been important to her. She worries a lot about it.
Therapist: So how might that influence how she experiences life now?
R: Maybe she still worries about it? But we've got plenty of food in our home.
K: But Roger, we've always tried to control her access to food, and we get angry when she steals it. Maybe she's just scared.
T: OK, Kathy, if that's so, that your Keli is really worried or scared of being hungry and starved, because that is what life in Columbia was like, then maybe she's just trying to take care of herself. Maybe she's just wanting to be sure she has food when her expectation is that food may not be around when she is hungry. And when she got hungry in Columbia, she got REALLY hungry, she was starving.

R: Oh, I feel so bad; have we hurt her more?
K: (starts to cry) We were all wrong. Oh our poor little Keli, what do we do now?
T: You feel badly that you didn't see this before and regret how you treated Keli.
K: Yes, I do. Is it too late?
T: Roger, how do you feel?
R: I feel terrible and (to Kathy) I think we can fix it?
K: Do you?
R: Yes.
T: I can feel how much you two want to help Keli and how regretful you are. You see what she is doing so differently now, through her experience, that makes sense to you?
K: Well, first of all, I think we need to make sure she has food around her and that we give her what she may be needing so that she can really know we will take care of her.
T: Maybe her intention wasn't to steal; maybe her intention was to try to get what she thinks she needs and wants for herself since she hadn't experienced caregivers as caring or giving.
R: That must be it. (Laughing) Now, if I can just keep remembering that, I won't be so angry when I find a yogurt container in her room.

In this example, if the parents assume that Keli is a thief and intends to steal from others what isn't hers, the parents will feel one way and act accordingly. If we help the parents to have *kind attributions*, and understand that all behavior is adaptive and has meaning, then the parents can look below the surface to see how Keli's taking food and hoarding may have nothing to do with stealing and have everything to do with a deep fear, grounded in her life experience, of starving. This will lead the parents to feel quite differently and act quite differently. This difference will help create a greater sense of safety and security for Keli, who will then be more likely to begin to incorporate these new experiences into her internal working models of caregivers.

Creating this safe base and having the sort of interactions described above can be quite difficult when the child is in school for most of the child's waking hours. That is why it may be very helpful, using this model of treatment and parenting, to have the child at home with the parent on a full-time basis and have the school provide a tutor for as long as treatment requires this arrangement (Becker-Weidman & Shell, 2010).

There are several other important elements of attachment-facilitating parenting that are grounded in Dyadic Developmental Psychotherapy that the therapist will want to communicate to the parents. Parents can certainly learn these various elements by reading books or articles, and therapists can "train" parents using psycho-educational models. However, early in treatment, and this is when the material is imparted, it is useful to remember that the therapist's focus is on building and maintaining a secure base. At times this is just telling the caregivers what to do and why it can be effective. Often, even within that first session, the parents feel enough safety and comfort that direct instruction is appreciated and effective. However, frequently there are times when the therapist will find it therapeutic to evoke the material and principles from the parents by exploring with the parents what is their thinking, their feeling states, their experiences as parents, and how they understand their child. Using PACE and follow-lead-follow, the therapist can explore all of these areas and help parents come to a deeper understanding of themselves and of their child.

All of the components of Dyadic Developmental Psychotherapy previously described are essential in the therapist's work with the parents. These same components are also essential elements of attachment-facilitating parenting. PLACE, creating positive concordant intersubjective experiences, follow-lead-follow, and the affective/reflective dialogue, for example, are all necessary and essential ingredients of attachment-facilitating parenting. Other considerations for parenting that the therapist can help parents with include the following:

- Parent the child in accordance with the child's developmental age and functioning.
- Avoid power struggles and other interactions that put the parent and child at odds with each other. Parents set the rhythm, tone, and emotional quality of the relationship and experience without being controlling (no threats, bribes, or force).

The Dyadic Developmental Psychotherapy components and principles of attunement (one element of intersubjectivity), use of self, insightfulness, reflection, and sensitivity, among others, lead parents to appreciate that their interactions with their child must be sensitive to the child's unique experience. Parents are encouraged to recognize how element of the child's past experiences may continue to affect the child and the impact of these experiences on development. Children with significant histories of trauma and maltreatment function at a developmentally younger age than their chronological age (Becker-Weidman, 2009). Sensitive, responsive parenting that is consistent with Dyadic Developmental Psychotherapy responds to this discrepancy between developmental and chronological age by encouraging parents to respond to and interact with their child in developmentally appropriate ways. Interacting with the child in ways that are sensitive to the child's developmental functioning will often avoid and eliminate many sources of bad feelings between parent and child. Asking a child who is developmentally younger than the child's chronological age to "act your age" is clearly a recipe for disaster. The parent will be frustrated and upset and so will the child. The therapist can help parents by helping them appreciate that treating the child at the child's developmental age is protective and helps to avoid putting the child in difficult situations. Understanding the child's developmental age and interacting accordingly in a sensitive manner is another way for the parent to go deeper into understanding their child and changing the lens through which the parent views the child.

WOUNDED PARENTS

Therapists practicing Dyadic Developmental Psychotherapy will find themselves working with wounded parents whose difficulties may range from minor to very significant and severe. In this section I will briefly touch on some ideas that therapists practicing within the Dyadic Developmental Psychotherapy framework may find helpful. For a detailed account of how to help these parents, there are a number of good articles and texts (Becker-Weidman & Shell, 2010; Shell, 2005/2008). One important consideration is the attachment style of the caregiver. Considering what is the person's attachment style can help a therapist consider how to approach that person. The basic tenants of Dyadic Developmental Psychotherapy apply to working with wounded parents just as these principles and methods apply to work with children. The therapist must begin by developing a trusting emotionally authentic relationship: Building the Alliance and then, Maintaining the Alliance. Helping create a safe therapeutic setting, which will involve co-regulating affect, is necessary for building an alliance. Building and maintaining an alliance may involve putting considerable time and effort into the affective/reflective dialogue and co-regulating affect. Caregivers with an unresolved trauma history or other difficulties require more time to feel safe with the therapist, and so the therapist may find that more time than is typical is spent seeing only the parents and the pace is slower. It is vital that the therapist focuses on the process and not become impatient to "get to the good stuff" with the family and child before the caregivers are ready to create safety for the child. Building and maintaining an alliance with caregivers and helping them experience the value and healing power of the affective/reflective dialogue is therapeutic in and of itself. The experience of "feeling felt" emotionally and psychologically is a very powerful therapeutic agent.

While telling parents what to do and how to do it may seem like an expedient solution to the difficulties of working with wounded parents, it is not. While teaching someone to "fish" takes much longer than just giving them the "fish," learning to fish will, in the long run, increase their sense of efficacy, self-concept, and competency. Whatever the therapist wants the caregiver to be able to do with the child, the therapist has to be able to do with the parent. Modeling and creating the experiences with the parent that the therapist wishes the parent to create with the child is much more powerful and long-lasting than providing a lecture on what to do. When caregivers discover their capacities and explore new ways of relating and being, the parent is much more likely to "own" the experience and for these new ways of being (these changed internal working models) to become integrated into the person's autobiographical narrative.

In one session toward the end of treatment, I wondered with a parent why it was that he did not feel criticized or discouraged when so often he came away from sessions with a different way of seeing and doing. His response reflects how the use of the affective/reflective dialogue early in work with parents can very quickly create the safety necessary to build an alliance, explore, integrate, and heal.

Grandparents Barbara and Joe are seated on the couch, with granddaughter Tina seated between them. Tina has been in their home since the age of two. She was eighteen now. The family came into treatment nearly two years ago because of Tina's immaturity, school problems, temper tantrums, and inability to form peer relationships. The family was nearing the end of treatment, and in this session we were reflecting on the treatment experience.

Art: What I'm curious about is that you were saying, Joe, that I might make suggestions or have you think about how to do things better. So, one of the things I'm curious about is how did that happen in a way that didn't make you feel either guilty or bad about what you had been doing. In other words, I understand what you have been saying. I would say "Oh, try this." or "When Tina does this, you might want to think about this." I'm just wondering what didn't make you feel, "Every time we go there we're criticized, we're blamed, we're told that nothing we do is right." I'm just curious about that.
Joe: Well, for me in the logic that I use is, uh, the things that we were doing with Tina we had done with our three previous kids and it worked for them . . .
Art: Yeah . . .
Joe: . . . everything had worked pretty well for them.
Art: Yeah.
Joe: So we knew it can't be all bad.
Art: Yeah.
Joe: But you know, when you gave the analogy that the bonds and the relationships that are in the first few years of life didn't exist for Tina and she was like a house built on sand, because we had trouble initially, if you will recall, we had trouble understanding why we're giving her love and affection and all these other things . . .

Art: And for *years*, for years you've been doing it . . .
Joe: Yeah, and it isn't working . . .
Art: Yeah.
Joe: . . . so it was a case where *we* didn't know what to do in terms of what was going on so we're like an open book in that relationship . . .
Barbara: I think we just wanted to learn.
Joe: And then when you gave the analogy that hers was a house built on sand, so the foundation is crumbling and collapsing and you need to get that foundation going and built up from there, then it was a case where the door is open now, to be open for anything and for us. Our outlook was positive.
Art: How so?
Joe: And as I said, I think in our first meeting or so, you know, we had basically figured that we had three years that Tina is going to be with us before she left the home and her current condition then, what we saw, is her having an existence in a cardboard box. And we knew that she was capable of living better than that, and we wanted more for her . . .
Art: I see . . .
Joe: . . . so in our, in Barbara's and my mind, it was the case of, you know, we need to do what it takes so that Tina's going to be a success, 'cause you want the best for your kids, no matter what you do, and . . .
Art: Yeah.
Joe: . . . and with that as our primary goal and looking for what's best for Tina and what she's capable of achieving and doing that stuff which s*he* is, now more so than ever. You know, there wasn't any real guilt on our part . . .
Art: I see . . .
Barbara: I think we were just . . .
Joe: We're open; we're more open to suggestions . . .
Barbara: . . . because we knew what we were doing was not working.
Joe: We knew what *we* were doing was not working and that analogy about the house being built on sand so that the foundation was shaky, making everything we built on top of it shaky, explained it for me.
Art: And you wanted the best for your daughter.
Joe: So we just heard what you said as you trying to help us and . . .
Barbara: I always felt you were helping us be better parents for Tina.
Joe: Yeah, we just knew you were with us trying to help us.

A Few Thoughts About the First Meetings with Parents

Since it is much easier to address pitfalls before they occur than after, I have found that there are several topics that I come to with parents in the first meetings with them. While some of this material is covered in a discussion, much of it is conveyed experientially. PACE is very important, as is the affective/reflective dialogue. These and the other components of Dyadic Developmental Psychotherapy guide the therapist's work with the family. The therapist would like parents to begin to think about and use PLACE and the affective/reflective dialogue with their child as soon as possible. The therapist will want the parents to begin to explore the notion that behavior has meaning and purpose and that the parents and therapist need to go deeper (being an ACE parent) to discover that with the child. It is necessary for the parent to consider what is causing or motivating the child's behavior, to be able to see and experience though the child's eyes.

The types of experiences that the therapist wants parents to create and have with their child take time. Being in school most of the day can distract, dilute, or even undercut the parent's ability to create these experiences and to create a safe PLACE at home. For that reason the therapist may find it very helpful to bring up the issue of the parent keeping the child at home with the school district providing a tutor. While this is clearly not an essential element of Dyadic Developmental Psychotherapy, it does advance the work very well and is something to be considered by the therapist.

An early discussion, or at least a mention of how the caregiver's "buttons" may be recognized during treatment to help the parent be more of the type of parent he or she would like to be is another topic best touched on early in work with the parents. This can be addressed during the assessment when the therapist may ask the caregivers, "Of all the things your child does, what most gets under your skin, or irritates or annoys you?" The therapist can then ask, "What do you think it is about you or your background that makes (the thing that the parent finds most disturbing) so disturbing/annoying/irritating to you?" By beginning to consider this and explore it early in treatment, it then becomes a normal part of what the therapist and parent discuss during treatment.

The therapist may also find it helpful when parents understand the therapist's intentions. This can be done by being explicit about those intentions. For example, the therapist's understanding of "Why are we all here?" can be made explicit. Generally the therapist and family are getting together because the parents and family would like the family to be a happier place. If that is one of the parent's intentions, then if the therapist sees something happening in a session that is not supportive of that intention, the therapist may want to act. The therapist may want to have a discussion similar to the following with parents before starting to see the child.

Therapist: Now, you indicated that you and your family are here to make the family a happier place, among other reasons, do I have that right?
Mr. Dante: Yes, that's right. The Dante home isn't very happy right now.
Mrs. Dante: We want to know what to do to help Jeremy.
T: Ok, so if I see something starting in the session with Jer that I think might not be helpful or might not get us where you want to be, is it ok if I interrupt you? Or would you find that disrespectful or rude?

Mr. D: (smiling) Hell no. Just take your shoe off and throw it at me.
T: (laughing) Well, I don't think I'd do that, but would it be OK if I just said, (holding up my hand like a stop sign) "hang on a moment"?
Mrs. D & Mr. D: Sure
T: If I do that it would only be because I thought interrupting would be helpful. We'd talk about it after the session with Jer so that I'd know if it had been OK and we can talk about what happened and why. How does that sound?
Mr. D: That's good. OK.

Another principle that can be helpful to have illustrated early in the therapist's meetings with parents is, "It's about connections not compliance." This is a concept that is intrinsic to the practice of Dyadic Developmental Psychotherapy. While behavior is certainly important, the therapist practicing Dyadic Developmental Psychotherapy and working with parents will always be curious about the meaning of the behavior to the child and the parents. The therapist will want to go deeper and even co-create new meanings that integrate into the autobiographical narrative in a healing and freeing way. Many parents come to the therapist wanting to know how to stop a behavior, get the child to listen, to make his bed, brush her teeth, stop telling lies, etc. The parents want to find ways to increase compliance. The therapist practicing Dyadic Developmental Psychotherapy recognizes that compliance certainly has a place in families, at school, and in the community, and the way to get there is through the relationship; it's about connections not compliance. Forcing compliance does not secure compliance. Building a meaningful and deep relationship, the connection, that leads to "compliance." The therapist can demonstrate this by focusing the work with parents on building a relationship with the parents, developing the affective/reflective dialogue, being accepting and curious, and by having lots of empathy for the family. It is through the therapist's connection with the caregivers that the therapist will impart many of these principles in a way that caregivers can use.

How all the above topics are woven into the session(s) with the caregiver will reflect the therapist's own use of self and particular style. Some may be casually mentioned, such as the discussion about interrupting if necessary, while others can be explored with the parents as they make discoveries on their own with the therapist.

SUMMARY AND CONCLUSIONS

This brief chapter provides the Dyadic Developmental Psychotherapy psychotherapist with some concepts and principles for helping caregivers begin creating attachment-facilitating experiences with their child in a way that is consistent with the principles and methods of Dyadic Developmental Psychotherapy. PACE, affective/reflective dialogue, going deeper, co-regulation of affect, and other components are all elements of Dyadic Developmental Psychotherapy that the therapist can implement with parents in the same way that the therapist wants the parents to implement with their child.

Several concepts were described that can help parents better understand their children and build a better relationship. *All behavior is adaptive and has meaning* and *kind attributions* are two of these concepts. Both of these, along with the various components of Dyadic Developmental Psychotherapy help create a safe PLACE at home that will facilitate exploration, integration, and healing. Another important concept for therapists to keep in mind and to help caregivers with is the idea that many children who have experienced chronic maltreatment are developmentally younger than their chronological age and this must be taken into account when interacting with the child. When therapists help caregivers gain an appreciation of these concepts, parents are better able to set the emotional tone and rhythm of the family.

Communicating these concepts and other dimensions of attachment-facilitating parenting with caregivers can be a challenge. While it may be tempting to give a quick talk or lecture on the material, often the therapist may find it more helpful to evoke the material using ACE and exploring the parent's perceptions and understandings.

Working with wounded parents is a challenge for therapists, especially when there is a child at risk in the home. While it may be tempting to tell the parents what to do, how, and why, the therapist will be more successful in the long run by first focusing on building an alliance with the parents. Wounded parents need more PACE and positive concordant intersubjective experiences with the therapist. The therapist will need to take more time to create safety so that exploration can occur at the parent's pace.

Helping parents better understand their children by changing the lens through which they view their children is an important approach to building and maintain the alliance. As caregivers find that these new ways of thinking, feeling, and acting produce better relationships that more closely match their hopes and dreams for their family, the deeper they are willing to go in exploration of their child's world and their own life history and experiences. Ultimately, this leads to a richer integration of experience and healing for the family. It's about connections not compliance.

Chapter 8

Conclusion and Summary

By now the reader should have a good understanding of the practice, principles, and methods of Dyadic Developmental Psychotherapy, an evidence-based, effective, and empirically validated treatment. At the core of Dyadic Developmental Psychotherapy is the therapist attitude of PACE (Playful, Accepting, Curious, and Empathic). The model, developed by Daniel Hughes, can be used in family and individual treatment, with children, adolescents, and adults. In this book I have focused primarily on working with families, parents, and youth, but the model has broader utility and has been expanded by Hughes to be an Attachment Focused Family Therapy (Hughes, 2007).

While securing a thorough assessment is not an intrinsic part of Dyadic Developmental Psychotherapy, it is good clinical practice to conduct one. The assessment process itself can provide the family with a therapeutic experience. As the therapist explores not only the child's history and functioning, but also the caregiver's perceptions, experiences, and thinking, the therapist is demonstrating many components of Dyadic Developmental Psychotherapy, such as PACE, follow-lead-follow, and the importance of going deeper into what may be causing behavior, that all behavior has meaning and is adaptive, as well as the value of having kind attributions. Conducting a thorough assessment facilitates the identification of important issues that may be a factor in the current situation, such as sensory-integration, neuropsychological dysfunction, cognitive functioning, and developmental age and functioning. Chronic early maltreatment within a caregiving relationship and complex trauma can result in impairment in various domains. When the therapist conducts such an assessment, the therapist is demonstrating that the therapist is interested in causes, not merely surface symptoms. It does matter a lot what is causing a child's attention problems. The "theory of mind" that the caregivers have of the cause will lead the caregivers to feel and act in particular ways that may or may not be helpful. For example, if the parents believe the child's attention problems are caused by the child's not being respectful or caring, they will feel and act very differently than if they understand the attention problems to be the result of prenatal exposure to alcohol causing cognitive impairments.

An important element in assessment is assessing the caregiver's capacity to create a healing PLACE at home. This involves the parent's commitment, sensitivity, insightfulness, and reflective function. While there are several formal methodologies that can be used to assess these dimensions, therapists can use their clinical judgment to informally assess these dimensions. The use of the Adult Attachment Interview as a clinical tool was described as a useful adjunct to assessment. Understanding a caregiver's pattern of attachment provides the therapist with valuable information about how to build and maintain an alliance with that caregiver. Insightfulness is an important quality for caregivers to have if they are to be therapeutic and helpful. Insightfulness, the ability to reflect on one's own experiences, the experiences of others, and the relationship, can be learned and developed, so understanding a caregiver's current capacity can influence how treatment proceeds. Insightfulness can be informally assessed throughout treatment as the therapist notices how the caregiver interprets and responds to different experiences in the treatment setting. Parent commitment is the best predictor of placement stability in foster care (Dozier & Lindheim, 2006). It is also a strong predictor of how treatment may proceed. Parents who feel overwhelmed and who have a lower commitment to their child may need much more support. It is helpful if the therapist does not try to convince the parents regarding their placement decisions; this needs to be the family's decision. What the parents do need is an "ACE" therapist, one who can accept their feelings and perceptions, one who is curious about these, and one who can provide empathy. It is always important to remember, Parents = Keystone. Parents are the keystone of treatment outcome.

The elements of Dyadic Developmental Psychotherapy include affect arousal, forming and maintain a therapeutic alliance, acceptance and empathy, interactive repair, and intersubjectivity. Fourteen components were described in detail. These components include:

1. Therapist use of self
2. Process focused: It's about connections not compliance
3. PLACE & PACE (Playful, Loving, Accepting, Curious, Empathy & Playful, Accepting, Curious, Empathy)
4. Intersubjectivity

5. Reflective Capacity
6. Affective/Reflective dialogue
7. Commitment
8. Insightfulness
9. Coherent Narrative
10. Co-regulation of emotions
11. Co-creation of meaning
12. Follow-lead-follow
13. Interactive repair
14. Nonverbal-verbal dialogue

Which component is used to a greater or lesser degree depends in part on the relational processes evident at that moment, the nature and quality of the relationships in the treatment setting, and on the phase of treatment evident at that moment in treatment.

The section on phases of treatment is grounded in attachment theory, which is the foundation of Dyadic Developmental Psychotherapy. These phases are Alliance (safe base), Exploration, Integration, and Healing. I break the Alliance phase into creating an alliance and then maintaining an alliance because of the overlapping and cyclical nature of these phases. The alliance or secure base provides safety, which is necessary for exploration. Maintaining the alliance and interactive repair, a component of Dyadic Developmental Psychotherapy, occurs throughout treatment. Safety precedes exploration. Without safety, exploration cannot occur, and exploration is necessary for integration, which leads to healing. These phases occur in an overlapping and cyclical manner. The family can experience exploration, integration, and healing all within the first session. Over time and throughout treatment, these experiences will be deepened and further developed. Within this framework the therapist can see, and clinical experience verifies, that the nature and quality of the therapeutic relationship changes over time. There are both qualitative and quantitative differences between different points in the treatment process. Trust evolves throughout treatment. There can be several phases occurring within one session, and there may be one phase primarily in evidence across several sessions.

The fourteen components of Dyadic Developmental Psychotherapy are used throughout treatment but do tend to be used in a different mix, depending on the experience occurring at that moment or in that phase of treatment. So, for example, while PACE and intersubjectivity are used throughout treatment, when building and maintain the alliance, follow-lead-follow and co-regulation of affect may take on greater prominence. Once a therapeutic alliance has been formed, the therapist can proceed to deepen and strengthen this alliance. When working on maintaining the alliance, the components of follow-lead-follow, interactive repair, and co-regulation of affect take on greater importance. Once there is some safety present in the therapy setting and a secure base is being established, exploration begins and deepens over time. Exploration presents many challenges for the therapist practicing Dyadic Developmental Psychotherapy. The primary task is to create experiences with real emotion while avoiding dysregulating the client. This phase is characterized by deeper exploration of past traumas and the evoking of affect associated with those experiences in a titrated manner to facilitate integration. A few components may take on greater significant during this phase. These are creating positive concordant intersubjective experiences, the reflective function, insightfulness, follow-lead-follow, interactive repair, commitment, co-creation of meaning and the co-regulation of affect. Exploration occurs though out treatment in a spiral, becoming deeper and taking on greater complexity over time. Integration is a process or phase that occurs to a greater or lesser degree throughout treatment. During this phase the therapist will notice the development of a coherent autobiographical narrative beginning and advancing. When focusing on integration, the components of affective/reflective dialogue and co-creation of meaning may take on greater prominence in the therapist's work. In many respects, healing begins when treatment begins, with the first contact with the therapist. This phase overlaps the other phases and occurs throughout treatment. The components of co-creation of new meanings, insightfulness and reflection, and affective/reflective dialogue may become more prominent during this phase.

The two chapters about parents and primary caregivers underscore the important idea that Parents = Keystone. Caregivers are the central element powerfully influencing how treatment proceeds. Parents are central to treatment success. This is because trauma and attachment disorders are primarily relational in nature, so treatment must by necessity also be relational. The difficulties being treated using Dyadic Developmental Psychotherapy are largely found within relationships. One of the principles of Dyadic Developmental Psychotherapy is that the therapist must build a primary relationship with the caregivers. As the therapist goes about developing an alliance with the parents, the therapist is assessing various parent capacities. Therapeutic parenting is grounded in the creation of a healing PLACE at home, the creation of a secure base that provides safety for the child. The capacities necessary for this include the capacity to be reflective, insightful and sensitive, and committed. These capacities can be assessed using formal methodologies, which were described in the chapter on the primacy of parents or using more informal clinically informed approaches. Most often, the therapist will rely on a less formal approach to reach clinical conclusions that can guide the therapists work. Insightfulness is an important capacity for caregivers. This is the capacity of the caregiver to see the other's point of view and appreciate the other's experience, which may be quite different than the caregiver's experience. The ability to be insightful is related to the construct of reflective function described by Fonagy et al. (2002). Commitment is, in some ways, related to the "L" in healing PLACE. Commitment is an important dimension in treatment since the best predictor of placement stability is the caregiver's commitment.

The caregiver's pattern of attachment is another important factor in shaping how the therapist will proceed with the family. The therapist is usually able to move more quickly with parents whose state of mind with respect to attachment is largely secure. Parents with insecure patterns of attachment will require more time for the therapist to build an alliance with them and for them to be able to create a therapeutic environment at home. Wounded parents and those with a disorganized state of mind with respect to attachment will require substantially more therapeutic intervention by the therapist, using all the various components of Dyadic Developmental Psychotherapy. Building the alliance necessary to do exploration, integration, and healing with these parents can take a considerable amount of time and effort. A potential danger for the therapist in these instances is moving too quickly into family work with the child and delving into the trauma when the parents are not able to provide the security and safety necessary for the child to expose these deep vulnerabilities. The Adult Attachment Interview provides a methodology to assess an adult's pattern of attachment. The questions in this interview provide very rich clinical data and can be very useful in assessing parents.

The chapter titled "Parents are the Keystone" briefly described working with parents to help create the healing PLACE necessary for exploration, integration, and healing. Building an alliance with the parents begins with the first contact with the family. Using PACE, follow-lead-follow, and creating concordant intersubjectivity are important components in building this alliance. Early in work with caregivers there are certain principles that we would like to develop. These include the principles that *all behavior is adaptive and has meaning*, and *kind attributions*. Kind attributions involves considering what may be underneath the behavior and attributing benign intentions to the child. These two principles help caregivers experience the child in very new and different ways that lead the parents to feel quite differently and then act in a more therapeutic manner. Leading the caregivers deeper into the child's experience enables the parents to feel empathy for the child, which is an important element in providing the safety necessary for exploration. Another important principle to communicate to caregivers is "It's about connections not compliance." This principle is grounded in the concept, from attachment theory, that it is through the attachment with a primary caregiver that a child develops emotional and behavioral control, internalizes values, beliefs, and morals, and experiences pleasure when pleasing caregivers. It is in connections, emotionally meaningful relationships, that "compliance" is rooted.

While there are many methods for helping grasp these principles, when caregivers discover the principles within the context of an accepting and encouraging concordant intersubjective experience with the therapist, the caregivers are much more likely to be able to integrate these principles into their every-day parenting. An important principle for caregivers to appreciate is that quite frequently children who have experienced complex trauma function at a developmental age significantly younger than their chronological age. This finding (Becker-Weidman, 2009) has important implications for treatment and parenting. Engaging the child in ways that are sensitive and responsive to the child's developmental functioning often eliminates or reduces many sources of conflict and stress in the parent-child relationship.

CERTIFICATION

Certification as a Dyadic Developmental Psychotherapy therapist provides the recognition that the therapist is practicing Dyadic Developmental Psychotherapy in a manner consistent with the standards of the Dyadic Developmental Psychotherapy Institute. This book describes the essential principles and methods of Dyadic Developmental Psychotherapy that are consistent with the Institute's standards, along with other elements of good practice.

The standards for certification as a Dyadic Developmental Psychotherapist are described on the Institute's website (http://www.dyadicdevelopmentalpsychotherapy.org/). To become certified, the applicant must apply and must meet certain prerequisites. These prerequisites include the following:

- Be a licensed, certified, or registered professional in the jurisdiction within which the professional is practicing.
- Have a strong background in working with children and families and a thorough knowledge of complex trauma and principles of attachment.
- Have malpractice insurance.
- Complete a minimum of 56 hours of training in Dyadic Developmental Psychotherapy in workshops led by a Certified Dyadic Developmental Psychotherapy Trainer.
- Two full sessions of Dyadic Developmental Psychotherapy treatment are required to be submitted as part of the application.

When the application is accepted, the applicant begins the practicum. The practicum is designed to advance the applications skills in applying the components of Dyadic Developmental Psychotherapy. During the practicum, the applicant will work with a Certified Dyadic Developmental Psychotherapy Consultant, who will review the applicants work and make recommendations to the Institute regarding the applicant's progress and certification. The requirements of the practicum include the following:

- Complete a minimum of one hundred sessions covering a minimum of ten cases using Dyadic Developmental Psychotherapy.
- Ten sessions must be submitted to the Dyadic Developmental Psychotherapy Institute Consultant for review. The applicant will receive written feedback by the consultant. After the first five tapes are reviewed, if the consultant recommends that the applicant continue the practicum, then a second consultant will review the first tape presented, along with the consultant's written report. If both consultants approve the applicant, then the next five sessions are reviewed by the consultant. The final session, along with the supervisor's written report, is then reviewed by a second consultant, and if approved, the applicant is certified as a Certified Dyadic Developmental Psychotherapy therapist for three years.

To remain certified, the therapist must complete a continuing education requirement every three years. That continuing education requirement can be met in several different ways. The therapist can attend an Advanced Practice Seminar led by a certified Dyadic Developmental Psychotherapy Institute trainer. The therapist can also have six hours of documented consultation with a certified Dyadic Developmental Psychotherapy consultant. In addition to the continuing education requirement, the therapist must submit one treatment session for consultation with two Dyadic Developmental Psychotherapy Institute Consultants, one of whom has not previously reviewed a tape by the therapist.

My intention in writing this book was to provide therapists with a deeper understanding and appreciation of the practice of Dyadic Developmental Psychotherapy. While the practice of Dyadic Developmental Psychotherapy is primarily an experiential practice firmly grounded in immediate experience, learning how to practice this method and improving one's skills in this method requires an analytic approach in addition to the experiential elements to learning Dyadic Developmental Psychotherapy. In fact, learning about Dyadic Developmental Psychotherapy uses the same components as practicing Dyadic Developmental Psychotherapy, in particular, the affective/reflective dialogue. This book represents the reflective element of that component and complements the affective elements acquired in training, Master Classes, and workshops about Dyadic Developmental Psychotherapy.

References

ATTACh. 2009. *Attachment Focused Therapy: A Professional Practice Guide.*

———. 2008. *Therapeutic Parent Manual.*

Ackenbach, T. M. 1991. *Manual for the Child Behavior Checklist/4-18 and 1991 profile*. Burlington, VT: University of Vermont Department of Psychiatry.

Becker-Weidman, A. 2006a. "Treatment for Children with Trauma-Attachment Disorders: Dyadic Developmental Psychotherapy." *Child and Adolescent Social Work Journal*, 23 (2), 147–171.

———. 2006b. "Dyadic Developmental Psychotherapy: A Multi-Year Follow-Up." In *New Developments In Child Abuse Research*, ed. Stanley M. Sturt. New York: Nova Science Publishers, 43–60.

———. 2006c. *Principles of Attachment Parenting*. DVD. Williamsville, NY: Center For Family Development.

———. 2005, 2008. "The Logistics of Providing Dyadic Developmental Psychotherapy." Pp. 43–65 in *Creating Capacity for Attachment: Dyadic Developmental Psychotherapy in the Treatment of Trauma-Attachment Disorders,* ed. Arthur Becker-Weidman and Deborah Shell. Oklahoma City, OK: Wood'N'Barnes.

———. 2005, 2008. "Dyadic Developmental Psychotherapy: The Theory." Pp. 7–42 in *Creating Capacity for Attachment: Dyadic Developmental Psychotherapy in the Treatment of Trauma-Attachment Disorders*, ed. Arthur Becker-Weidman & Deborah Shell. Oklahoma City, OK: Wood'N'Barnes.

———. 2007. *Assessing Children with Complex Trauma & Disorders of Attachment.* DVD set. Brookfield, VT: Resourceful Recordings,

———. 2008. "Sensory-Integration Screener." Williamsville, NY: Center For Family Development, 2008, http://www.center4familydevelop.com/sensorychecklist.htm. Retrieved August 24, 2009.

———. 2009. "Effects of Early Maltreatment on Development: A Descriptive Study Using the Vineland." *Child Welfare*, 88 (2), 137–161.

———. 2010. *Assessing Caregiver Reflective Capacity, Commitment, Insightfulness, and Sensitivity*. DVD. Burlington VT: Resourceful Recordings.

Becker-Weidman, A., S. Becker-Weidman, B. Green, K. Hunt, and J. Walker. 2005, 2008. "By Parents: The Healing of Three Families." Pp. 235–287 in *Creating Capacity for Attachment: Dyadic Developmental Psychotherapy in the Treatment of Trauma-Attachment Disorders,* ed. Arthur Becker-Weidman and Deborah Shell. Oklahoma City, OK: Wood'N'Barnes.

Becker-Weidman, A., and D. Hughes. 2008. "Dyadic Developmental Psychotherapy: An Evidence-Based Treatment for Children with Complex Trauma and Disorders of Attachment." *Child & Family Social Work*, 13, 329–337.

Becker-Weidman, A., and Deborah Shell, Deborah (eds.). 2005. *Creating Capacity for Attachment: Dyadic Developmental Psychotherapy in the Treatment of Trauma-Attachment Disorders*. Oklahoma City, OK: Wood'N'Barnes.

———. 2010. *Attachment Parenting: Developing Connections and Healing Children*. Lanham, MD: Jason Aronson.

Bowlby, J. 1988. *A Secure Base*. New York: Basic Books.

———. 1980. *Attachment, Separation, and Loss*. New York: Basic Books.

Briere, J. 2002. "Treating Adult Survivors of Severe Childhood Abuse and Neglect: Further Development of an Integrative Model." In J. E. B. Meyers, L. Berliner, J. Briere, C. T. Hendrix, Reid, T. & C. Jenny (Eds.), *The APSAC Handbook on Child Maltreatment*, 2nd Ed. Newbury Park, CA: Sage Publications.

Briere, J., and C. Scott (Eds.). 2006. *Principles of Trauma Therapy*. Thousand Oaks, CA: Sage.

Bretherton, I., D. Ridgeway, and J. Cassidy. 1990. "Assessing Internal Working Models of the Attachment Relationship: An Attachment Story Completion Task." Pp. 272–308 in *Attachment in the Preschool Years: Theory, Research, and Intervention,* ed. Mark Greenbert, Dante Cicchetti, & Mark Cummings. Chicago: The University of Chicago Press.

Buck, J., and W. Warren. 1995. *House-Tree-Person Projective Drawing Technique: Manual and Interpretive Guide*, Los Angeles: Western Psychological Services.

Cassidy, J., and P. Shaver (Eds.). 2008. *Handbook of Attachment Theory, Research, and Clinical Applications 2nd Ed.* NY: Guilford.

Cook, A., M. Blaustein, J. Spinazolla, and B. van der Kolk. 2003. "Complex Trauma" in *Children and Adolescents.White Paper from the National Child Traumatic Stress Network Complex Trauma Task Force*. Los Angeles, CA: National Center for Child Traumatic Stress,

Cook, A., J. Spinazzola, J. Ford, C. Lanktree, M. Blaustein, M. Cloitre, et al. 2005. "Complex Trauma in Children and Adolescents." *Psychiatric Annals*, 35, 390–398.

Craven, P., and R. Lee. 2006. "Therapeutic Interventions for Foster Children: A Systematic Research Synthesis." *Research on Social Work Practice*, 16, 287–304.

Crowell, J., and G. Owens. 1998. *Manual For The Current Relationship Interview And Scoring System*. Version 4. http://ww.psychology.sunysb.edu/attachment/measures/content/cri_manual.pdf. Retrieved March 7, 2010.

Dozier, M., K. C. Stovall, and K. Albus. "Attachment and Psychopathology in Adulthood." In J. Cassidy & P. Shaver (Eds.). 2009. *Handbook of Attachment.* Pp. 718–745. New York: Guilford Press.

Dozier, M., K. C. Stovall, K. E. Albus, and B. Bates. 2001. "Attachment for Infants in Foster Care: The Role of Caregiver State of Mind." *Child Development*, 70, 1467–1477.

Dozier, M., and O. Lindhiem. 2006. "This Is My Child: Differences among Foster Parents in Commitment to Their Young Children." *Child Maltreatment* 11 (4), 338–345.

Fonagy, P., G. Gergely, E. Jurist, and M. Target. 2002. *Affect Regulation, Mentalization, and the Development of the Self.* Other Press, NewYork.

Hesse, E. 2008. *The Adult Attachment Interview: Protocol, Method of Analysis, and Empirical Studies.* Pp. 552–598 in J. Cassidy and P. Shaver (Eds), *Handbook of Attachment: Theory, Research, and Clinical Applications*, New York: Guilford Press.

Holmes, J. 1993. *John Bowlby and Attachment Theory.* New York: Routledge.

Hudson, J. 2010. Personal Communication, April 16.

Hughes, D. 2004. "An Attachment-Based Treatment of Maltreated Children and Young People." *Attachment and Human Development*, 6, 263–278.

———. 2005. "The Development of Dyadic Developmental Psychotherapy." Pp. vii–xvii in *Creating Capacity for Attachment*, ed. Arthur Becker-Weidman & Deborah Shell. Oklahoma City, OK: Wood'N'Barnes.

———. 2006. *Building the Bonds of Attachment*, 2nd ed., Lanham, MD: Jason Aronson.

———. 2007. *Attachment-Focused Family Therapy.* NewYork: W.W. Norton.

———. 2009. *Attachment-Focused Parenting.* New York: W.W. Norton.

———. In press. *Attachment-Focused Family Therapy: The Workbook.* New York: W.W. Norton.

Koren-Karie, N., D. Oppenheim, S. Dolev, E. Sher, and E. Etzion-Carasso. 2002. "Mothers' Insightfulness Regarding Their Infants' Internal Experience: Relations with Maternal Sensitivity and Infant Attachment." *Developmental Psychology,* 38, 534–542.

Lambert, M. 2004. *Bergin and Garfield's Handbook of Psychotherapy and Behavior Change.* New York: Wiley.

Main, M. 1996. "Adult Attachment Interview Protocol." http://www.psychology.sunysb.edu/attachment/measures/content/aai_interview.pdf. Accessed March 7, 2010.

Mattson, A. 2010. "The Role of Neuropsychological Evaluation and Intervention in the Management and Treatment of Children with a History of Early Maltreatment," in A. Becker-Weidman & Deborah Shell (Eds.), *Attachment Parenting.* Lanham, MD: Jason Aronson.

O'Connor, T., and C. Zeanah. 2003. "Attachment Disorders: Assessment Strategies and Treatment Approaches." *Attachment & Human Development*, 5, 223–245.

Oppenheim, D., N. Koren-Karie, and A. Sagi. 2001. "Mothers' Empathic Understanding of Their Preschoolers' Internal Experience: Relations with Early Attachment." *International Journal of Behavioral Development,* 25, 16–26.

Oppenheim, D., and N. Koren-Karie. 2002. "Mothers' Insightfulness Regarding Their Children's Internal Worlds: The Capacity Underlying Secure Child-Mother Relationships." *Infant Mental Health Journal, 23(6),* 593–605.

Oppenheim, D., D. Goldsmith, and N. Koren-Karie. 2004. "Maternal Insightfulness and Preschoolers' Emotion and Behavior Problems: Reciprocal Influences in a Therapeutic Preschool Program." *Infant Mental Health Journal*, 352-367, 25.

Ring, M. 2005. "For Parents." Pp. 216–234 in A. Becker-Weidman & D. Shell (Eds), *Creating Capacity for Attachment: Dyadic Developmental Psychotherapy in the Treatment of Trauma-Attachment Disorders.* Oklahoma City, OK: Wood'N'Barnes.

Saunders, B., L. Berliner, and R. Hanson. 2004. *Child Physical and Sexual Abuse: Guidelines for Treatment.* http://academicdepartments.musc.edu/ncvc/resources_prof/OVC_guidelines04-26-04.pdf. Accessed March 20, 2010.

Shell, D. 2005. "Dyadic Developmental Psychotherapy: Working with Unresolved Parents." Pp. 109–129 in *Creating Capacity for Attachment: Dyadic Developmental Psychotherapy in the Treatment of Trauma-Attachment Disorders*, ed. Arthur Becker-Weidman & Deborah Shell. Oklahoma City, OK: Wood'N'Barnes.

Siegel, D. J. 1999. *The Developing Mind.* New York: Guilford Press.

———. 2002. "Toward an Interpersonal Neurobiology of the Developing Mind: Attachment Relationships, 'Mindsight,' and Neural Integration." *Infant Mental Health Journal*, 22, 67–94.

Steele, H., and M. Steele (Eds.). 2008. *Clinical Applications of the Adult Attachment Interview.* New York: Guilford Press.

Trevarthen, C. 2001. "Intrinsic Motives for Companionship in Understanding: Their Origin, Development, and Significance for Infant Mental Health." *Infant Mental Health Journal*, 22, 95–131.

Tronick, E. Z. 1989. "Emotions and Emotional Communication in Infants." *American Psychologist*, 44(2), 112–119.

———. 2005. "Why Is Connection with Others So Critical? The Formation of Dyadic States of Consciousness: Coherence Governed Selection and the Co-creation of Meaning out of Messy Meaning Making." Pp. 293–315 in J. Nadel and D. Muir (eds). *Emotional Development.* Oxford University Press.

Tyrell, C., M. Dozier, G. B. Teague, and R. Fallot. 1999. "Effective Treatment Relationships for Persons with Serious Psychiatric Disorders: The Importance of Attachment States of Mind." *Journal of Consulting and Clinical Psychology*, 67, 725–733.

Wenck, L. S. 1997. *House-Tree-Person Drawings: An Illustrated Diagnostic Handbook.* Los Angeles: Western Psychological Services.

Index

About the Author

Arthur Becker-Weidman, PhD received his MSW from the University of Maryland at Baltimore and his PhD from the University of Maryland's Institute for Child Study. He has achieved diplomate status in child psychology and forensic psychology from the American Board of Psychological Specialties. He is a registered clinician with the Association for the Treatment and Training in the Attachment of Children and is a certified therapist, consultant, and trainer in Dyadic Developmental Psychotherapy®©.

As Director of the Center For Family Development Dr. Becker-Weidman consults with governments, departments of social services, residential treatment centers, mental health clinics, and professionals throughout the United States, Canada, Singapore, Finland, Australia, the Czech Republic, and Slovakia. Dr. Becker-Weidman's work has focused on the evaluation and treatment of adopted and foster children and their families, Complex-Post Traumatic Stress Disorder, and Alcohol Related Neurological Dysfunction (Fetal Alcohol Spectrum Disorder or FAS). Dr. Becker-Weidman had an extensive practice consulting with professionals and clinics, using Skype. He provides training and consultation to therapists, other professionals, and parents throughout the United States and internationally.

Dr. Becker-Weidman is on the board of directors of the Association for the Treatment and Training in the Attachment of Children, serves as a vice-president for clinical issues, serves on the Research Committee and Training Committee, and chairs the Registration Committee. He is an adjunct clinical professor at the State University of New York at Buffalo. Dr. Becker-Weidman is President of the Board of the Dyadic Developmental Psychotherapy Institute®©.

Dr. Becker-Weidman has published over a dozen papers in peer-reviewed professional journals. He is the co-editor of the book, *Creating Capacity for Attachment*, published by Wood 'N' Barnes in 2005, second printing 2008. He is co-editor of the book, *Attachment Parenting*, Jason Aronson, 2010. Dr. Becker-Weidman's newest book, *The Dyadic Developmental Psychotherapy Casebook*, will be published by Jason Aronson in 2011. Dr. Becker-Weidman has several DVDs that are extensively used by professionals and parents: *Principles of Attachment Parenting* (2006), *Assessing Children with Complex Trauma and Disorders of Attachment* (2008), Assessing *Caregiver Reflective Capacity, Commitment, Insightfulness, & Sensitivity* (2010), and *Introduction to Dyadic Developmental Psychotherapy*, with Daniel Hughes (2010).

Aweidman@Concentric.net
www.Center4FamilyDevelop.com

www.ingramcontent.com/pod-product-compliance
Ingram Content Group UK Ltd.
Pitfield, Milton Keynes, MK11 3LW, UK
UKHW012041150926
475560UK00001B/118

9 780765 707932